18.36
S.D.
G.K. Hall

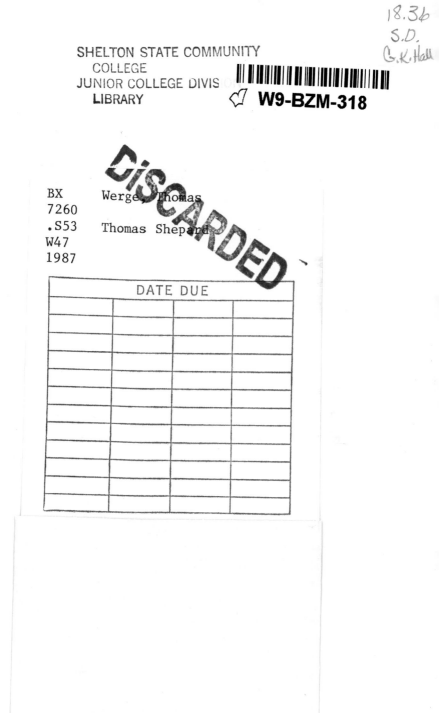

Werge, Thomas

Thomas Shepard

DATE DUE			

Thomas Shepard

Twayne's United States Authors Series

Pattie Cowell, Editor

Colorado State University

TUSAS 519

THE

Sound Beleever.

OR,

A TREATISE

OF

Evangelicall Converſion.

DISCOVERING

The work of Chriſts Spirit, in reconciling of a ſinner to God.

By THO: SHEPARD, ſometimes of *Emmanuel Colledge* in *Cambridge*, Now Preacher of Gods Word in NEW-ENGLAND.

MAT. 18. 11.

I came to ſave that which was loſt.

LONDON,

Printed for *R. Dawlman.* 1645.

Title page of Thomas Shepard's *The Sound Believer.*

By permission of the Houghton Library, Harvard University.

Thomas Shepard

By Thomas Werge

University of Notre Dame

Twayne Publishers
A Division of G. K. Hall & Co. • Boston

Thomas Shepard

Thomas Werge

Published by Twayne Publishers
A Division of G.K. Hall & Co.
70 Lincoln Street
Boston, Massachusetts 02111

Copyediting supervised by Lewis DeSimone
Book production by Janet Zietowski
Book design by Barbara Anderson

Typeset in 11 pt. Garamond
by Modern Graphics, Inc.,
Weymouth, Massachusetts

Printed on permanent/durable acid-free paper
and bound in the United States of America

Library of Congress Cataloging-in-Publication Data

Werge, Thomas.
Thomas Shepard.

(Twayne's United States authors series ; TUSAS 519)
Bibliography: p.
Includes index.
1. Shepard, Thomas, 1605–1649. I. Title. II. Series.
BX7260.S53W47 1987 285.8′092′4 87–8576
ISBN 0–8057–7507–2 (alk. paper)

for my mother and father and for Noelle

Contents

About the Author

Thomas Werge, professor of English at the University of Notre Dame, received his B.A. from Hope College and M.A. and Ph.D. from Cornell University. He is coauthor of *Early Puritan Writers* and has written on the religious and philosophical dimensions of American literature as well as on such figures as Dante and Dostoevski. His articles and reviews have appeared in such journals as *Early American Literature, ESQ, Studies in the Novel, NEQ,* and *Dante Studies.* He is currently coeditor of the journal *Religion and Literature,* published by the Notre Dame Department of English.

Preface

In his groundbreaking *History of American Literature, 1607–1765,* first published in 1878, Moses Coit Tyler wrote that of all the great Puritan preachers of early New England, three towered above the others: Thomas Hooker, John Cotton, and Thomas Shepard. Although they could be compared with each other, he added, "with them could be compared no one else." More than a century later, Tyler's judgment has been sustained. Yet while we have substantive studies on Cotton by Larzer Ziff and Everett H. Emerson and on Hooker by such scholars as Sargent Bush, Jr. and Frank Shuffleton, we have paid less attention to Shepard. From historical, literary, and religious perspectives, Shepard's importance is clear. His influence persisted. Shepard's life and writings dramatize the Puritan spirit and provide a compelling testament to the religious origins of America's experience.

Since these origins are to be found in part in the Puritan attempt to reform the Church of England not only in its liturgy but in the emphasis and direction of its doctrines, chapter 1 outlines Shepard's life in the setting of the Puritan movement in old and New England. The chapter concludes by treating his *Autobiography,* which dramatizes God's providential and salvific work as Shepard retrospectively interprets its presence in his experience. Chapter 2 discusses the roots of and precedents for Puritanism—particularly in Augustinianism and the Reformation—and considers the ways in which the American Puritans remain continuous with, yet diverge sharply from, these older forms of faith. The central place of polarities and dialectic in the Puritan vision—election and reprobation, light and darkness, Gospel and law, grace and nature, the City of God and the city of man, the covenant of grace and that of works—provides a key to an understanding of the Puritan conception of experience, language, and personal and communal salvation.

Chapters 3 through 6 explore Shepard's major writings. Although I often have arranged them chronologically within each chapter, I do not use a chronological order throughout. Rather, I treat each group of works as an expression, respectively, of Shepard's defense of the "New England Way" (chapter 3); his description and exposition, in major sermons, of the Puritan faith, doctrine, and vision (chapter 4); his three delineations of the relationship among conscience, real liberty, and the mediation of Christ addressed respectively to a general audience *(Subjection to Christ)*, to a specific friend *(Certain Select Cases Resolved)*, and to his own inward spirit in its dialectic with God *(Journal)* (chapter 5); and his dramatization of love and mercy as they contend with sin and despair in the individual soul and in the broader covenant between God and the saints (chapter 6). Chapter 7 considers his influence, in a personal as well as a representative way, on later American literature, thought, and culture. Shepard's preoccupations remain at once constant and complex, of course, so that the works treated in chapters 3 through 6 are interrelated. The headings I have used indicate particular emphases rather than rigid or exclusive categories.

Even apart from his writings, Shepard played an intense and formative role in New England. He journeyed among the Indians and attempted to reconcile the hostilities and tensions between Puritan culture and their own ways. He had a direct hand in the founding of Harvard College, in the turbulent events of the Antinomian controversy, and in the forming and sustaining of the first permanent congregation in Cambridge. As a minister, his pastoral efforts were tireless, and he was clearly devoted to his family. For the first generation of New England as for such a later commentator as Cotton Mather, Shepard's death at the age of forty-four was nothing less than calamitous and foreboding.

For all these important actions and personal strengths, it was the powerful efficacy of Shepard's sermons and other writings that led Jonathan Mitchel, his successor in the church at Cambridge, to speak of "the lively voice of this Soul-melting Preacher, whom [we] never can forget." The Puritan writer Edward Johnson described Shepard's ministry as "soul-ravishing" and Shepard himself as "a man of a thousand." The esteem in which readers held his work verifies that these epithets were not merely conventions. *The Sincere Convert* remained in print through many editions from its publication in 1641 through the early part of the nineteenth century; *The Sound Believer* enjoyed widespread and persistent popularity and respect; several of his lesser-known works were reprinted in the eighteenth century; *The Parable of the Ten Virgins* greatly influenced Jonathan Edwards; and John A. Albro's *Life of Thomas Shepard,* first published in 1847, was included in a three-volume edition of Shepard's *Works* that appeared six years later. More recently, Michael McGiffert has edited the *Journal* and *Autobiography* and George Selement and Bruce Woolley *Thomas Shepard's Confessions*.

In my consideration of the religious and doctrinal dimensions and underlying ideas of Shepard's works, I have tried to indicate how interwoven with them are Shepard's imagination and rhetoric. Like Augustine, Luther, and, later, Edwards, Shepard was moved to conversion by the efficacy of the Word. The intensity of his own language and imagery, whether terrifying or tender, witnesses to the serious and even apocalyptic significance, for good or evil, Shepard attributes to the word spoken and preached, read and heard.

Each treatment of one of Shepard's works has two parts: a brief discussion of its "setting" broadly construed as the immediate circumstances of its composition if known, or theological and literary backgrounds and influences, or especially relevant ideas or events, or all these considerations; and a discussion of the structure and substance of the work itself. For Shepard's life, I have relied largely on Albro and on Shepard's *Autobiography*. I have retained the spelling, punctuation, and capitalization of the editions cited. Except when noted, these are the first editions. But I have emended *u* to *v* wherever appropriate, so that "euen" in the original here becomes "even." McGiffert's edition of the *Autobiography* and *Journal* modernizes Shepard's spelling. Quotations from these two works constitute the only exceptions to my general practice. Several of the editions I have used are not easily accessible even on microfilm or microform. I hope that my attempt to ensure accuracy by retaining the language and accidentals of the original editions will encourage further reference to and use of Shepard's writings. His voice and works remain resonant.

Two final textual notes: I occasionally abbreviate a title and use it in parenthetical references. A key to these references heads the notes, while full titles and editions cited are provided in the primary sources in the selected bibliography. I have used modern spellings for the titles when citing them in my text (for example, *The Sound Believer*) and the original spellings in the bibliography (the frontispiece reproduces the title page of the 1645 edition).

Generous grants from the Institute for Scholarship in the Liberal Arts at the University of Notre Dame and the Penrose Fund of the American Philosophical Society enabled me to complete this study. The staffs of Notre Dame's Memorial Library, the Houghton Library at Harvard, the Boston Public Library, the Newberry Library, and the New York Public Library were immensely helpful to me. My friends and colleagues, including Michael Colacurcio, Walter R. Davis, Emory Elliott, Everett H. Emerson, and Lawrence Buell, provided generous assistance. For their patience, advice, and encouragement, I owe special thanks to James P. Dougherty, William J. Krier, Joseph X. Brennan, Thomas Schlereth, Edward A. Kline, and Nathan O. Hatch. I am also indebted to A. James Prins, Taylor Stoehr, and Jonathan Bishop. In the preparation of the manuscript, Margaret Jasiewicz, Susan Curtis, and Nancy Kegler excelled. To all these people and many others I am very grateful. To my wife, Noelle, our three children, Rob, and our entire family, I can never adequately express the depth of my gratitude.

Thomas Werge

University of Notre Dame

Chronology

1605 Thomas Shepard born 5 November in Towcester, Northamptonshire, the youngest of nine children. Orphaned at a young age, he is brought up by his brother.

1619 After attending school in Towcester, admitted as a pensioner to Emmanuel College, Cambridge.

1623 Receives his B.A.

1627 Receives M.A. Having been influenced by the preaching of John Preston, experienced conversion, and embraced Puritan teachings, he is ordained deacon and then priest. Resides in family of Thomas Weld, minister in Terling, Essex. Thomas Hooker is minister in neighboring Chelmsford.

1627–1630 Minister at Earles-Colne, Essex.

1630 Silenced and suspended for nonconformity by William Laud, then bishop of London.

1632 Chaplain in family of Sir Richard Darley, Buttercrambe, Yorkshire. Marries Margaret Touteville on 23 July.

1633 Accepts invitation to preach in Heddon, Northumberland. Laud alerts authorities and he is forced into hiding. Birth of son, Thomas. Resolves to go to New England.

1634 Sails for New England from Harwich, Essex. Ship driven back by storm. Son dies. Remains in hiding.

1635 Second son born, named Thomas after first-born. Sails in August for Boston and arrives 3 October. Removes to Newtown (Cambridge). Chosen pastor of church at Cambridge. Margaret dies.

1636 Instrumental in founding of Harvard College and locating it in Cambridge.

1637 Organizes Synod to combat Antinomianism. Marries Joanna Hooker, daughter of Thomas Hooker.

1638 Participates in Anne Hutchinson's church trial and sentencing.

1641 Birth of son, Samuel, another child having died shortly after birth. *The Sincere Convert.*

1644 During these years, makes journeys among Indians with John Eliot. Begins tradition of scholarships for needy students. Contributes to plans for church government in New England.

1645 *The Sound Believer.*

1646 Birth and death at four months of son, John. Joanna dies. Indian mission established at Cambridge.

1647 Synod accepts plan for church government as *(Cambridge) Platform* for Congregational churches in America. Marries Margaret Boradel.

1648 Birth of son, Jeremiah. *A Defense of the Answer.*

1649 Shepard dies 25 August and is buried at Cambridge.

1660 Posthumous publication of *The Parable of the Ten Virgins.*

1832 *Autobiography.*

Chapter One

Seeking the Kingdom: Shepard and the Wayfaring Saints

St. Augustine writes in *The City of God* that real saints, or believers in Christ, "will not refuse the discipline of this temporal life, in which they are schooled for life eternal; nor will they lament their experience of it, for the good things of earth they use as pilgrims who are not detained by them, and its ills either prove or improve them."[1] The Calvinist divine Charles Drelincourt, a contemporary of Thomas Shepard, stresses the same vision of life as pilgrimage: "Like the old patriarchs, the Citizens of Heaven seek their true country, that is to say a celestial one: and their appearance is like that of people who are ascending to the Jerusalem that is on high."[2] We seek an "eternal weight of glory," claims Shepard, and "the time is not long, but that we shall feele what now we doe but heare of, and see but a little of, as we use to doe of things afar off: We are here but strangers, and have *no abiding city,* we look for this *that hath foundations.*"[3] As wayfaring saints, the English Puritans of the sixteenth and seventeenth centuries moved in a linear path through the world yet moved inwardly and heavenward in seeking the Kingdom of God. Their pilgrimage assumes a spiral form, and their struggle against the world, the flesh, the devil, and hierarchical and centralized church structures and governance, whether Roman Catholic, Anglican, or even Presbyterian, is as rooted in the search for salvation as is that of Christian in Bunyan's *Pilgrim's Progress.* Although the City of God, their "true country," was a heavenly city for the Puritans, those who emigrated also sought its approximation on earth—in the visibly "gathered saints by calling," and in the promised land and wilderness of New England.

England

On the same November day in 1605 that Thomas Shepard was born, several conspirators, including Guy Fawkes, were discovered in the "Gunpowder Plot" to destroy Parliament while King James I and both Houses were in session. Shepard notes in the first sentence of his *Autobiography* that on "the powder treason day, and that very hour . . . wherein the Parliament should have been blown up by Popish priests, I was then born, which occasioned my father to give me this name Thomas, because he said I would hardly believe that ever any such wickedness should be attempted by men against so religious and good Parliament."[4] Not quite a century earlier, Pope Leo X had bestowed on King Henry VIII the title *Defensor Fidei,* Defender of the Faith, for writing in defense of the traditional church teaching on the validity of the seven sacraments and against Luther's insistence that only baptism and the Lord's Supper constituted true sacraments. But since that gesture of doctrinal solidarity, England's religious history, in all its ecclesiastical, theological, and political dimensions, had been divisive and turbulent. Henry denied the ultimate authority of the pope over the English, or Anglican, church; Thomas More died a martyr for his belief in the pope's authority; and the tensions between Roman Catholics and Protestants in the wake of the Reformation, on the Continent and in England, intensified. Within the Anglican church, conflicts grew and sharpened over the relation between Scripture and tradition as rules of faith, the use of Catholic ritual and images in the liturgy, and the real nature and source of hierarchy and authority.

Although the Reformation in England was deeply influenced by Calvinism, and the Thirty-nine Articles to which all Anglican ministers in the late sixteenth century had to subscribe were essentially Calvinist, these serious disputes and others related to them continued to fester. Many Anglicans who had agreed with Henry VIII's prohibition of Calvin's works, which he banned in 1542, sympathized with traditional Roman Catholic and now Anglo-Catholic forms and rituals: the liturgy of the Mass, a hierarchical and sacerdotal structure in the church, the use of vestments, such visible gestures of faith as kneeling and making the sign of the Cross, the veneration of saints, and a pervasively sacramental and communal expression of religious faith. Other Anglicans, known as Puritans, echoed Luther's emphasis on Scripture, grace, and faith—*sola scriptura, sola gratia, sola fide*—as the exclusive way to salvation. But they broke with Luther's use of many of the traditional forms and rituals of the Roman Catholic liturgy and instead turned to Calvinist, and especially Presbyterian, forms of worship and order. In seeking to simplify and "purify" the order of worship, these Presbyterian Puritans joined with another nascent movement within Puritanism that came to value a "congregational" rather than a Presbyterian church polity: nonhierarchical, noncentralized, and supportive of a high degree of autonomy for individual congregations. Both Presbyterians and those who came to be known as Congregationalists were united in their opposition to Roman Catholicism, to "high-church" Anglicanism, and to the Separatist movement as it would later be seen in the Pilgrims. Yet loyal as they were to the Anglican church, the conflicts and tensions within that church remained powerful throughout Henry's reign and preoccupied Elizabeth as she ascended the throne in 1558.

The "Elizabethan Settlement" of 1559 sought to condemn any movement sympathetic to separating entirely from the institutional Anglican church and to reconcile the demands of the reform-minded and even radical Puritans—some of whom wished to abolish ritual, vestments, the use of the Prayer Books of 1549 and 1552, the celebration of such holy days as Christmas, and the entire structure of the Anglican hierarchy—with those of the traditional Anglican bishops and other church officers. But the struggles continued between conservative Anglicans and radical Puritan Anglicans as well as between Puritans who viewed Calvin's Geneva as the model for their Presbyterian ideal of church government and those who envisioned a more "democratic" model—one they believed typified the polity of the primitive Christian church. United as these parties were against Roman Catholicism on the one hand and Separatism and the political and religious radicals they defined as Antinomians on the other, the differences within the Anglican church and between the Puritan movements were vexing and profound. The "settlement" had settled little.

James I became king in 1603, two years before Shepard's birth. In 1604, in response to the president of Corpus Christi College, Oxford, he convened a group of eminent scholars and divines to revise the Bible previously translated by Tyndale as well as the so-called "Bishops' Bible" (1568) into a new version. Although this "Authorized Version" (1611) was a result of the combined efforts of the "high" and "low" branches of the Anglican church, most "low-church" Puritans continued to use the sixteenth-century Calvinist version known as the Geneva Bible. James's gesture clearly stemmed from his desire to nurture an ecclesiastical and political peace as well as from his piety. But with the crowning of Charles I in 1625, the tensions and conflicts James had attempted to moderate broke into severe and open conflict.

Shepard's father, a grocer, appears to have been not only a loyal supporter of James I and the Parliament but, in Shepard's words, "a wise, prudent man" and a "peacemaker" of strong piety. He died when Shepard was about ten years old. Shepard's mother, who had died some six years earlier, seems to have been intensely religious, scrupulous, and caring: "My mother was a woman much afflicted in conscience, sometimes even unto . . . distraction of mind, yet was sweetly recovered again before she died, and I being the youngest she did bear exceeding great love to me and made many prayers for me" (38). As a child, and later in memory, Shepard valued these parental bonds as fully as St. Augustine valued his mother's presence. Yet death and isolation shattered Shepard's hope that they could be sustained: "I did pray very strongly and heartily for the life of my father and made some covenant, if God would do it, to serve him the better as knowing I would be left alone if he was gone. Yet the Lord took him away by death, and so I was left fatherless and motherless" (39).

The childhood years between his mother's and father's deaths witnessed Shepard's suffering as a consistent pattern. Just before her death, his mother sent Shepard to live with his grandparents in order to avoid a plague sweeping Towcester. Many of his father's family died in the plague. Neglected by his grandparents, Shepard was then sent to live in another town with his uncle, where he was somewhat happier. His father, now remarried, sent for Thomas, but his stepmother seemed "not to love me but incensed my father often against me"—though, he adds, "it may be that it was justly also for my childishness" (38). At this point Shepard began to attend the Free School in Towcester, whose schoolmaster seems the real-life model for the novelistic types so common in later English literature: "he was exceeding . . . cruel and would deal roughly with me and so discouraged me wholly from desire of learning that I remember I wished oftentimes myself in any condition to keep hogs or beasts rather than to go to school and learn" (38).

Yet "by God's good providence" Shepard's domestic, educational, and religious life emerged from these afflictions. John, the only survivor among Shepard's three brothers, took him in: "so I lived with this my eldest brother who showed much love unto me and unto whom I owe much, for him God made to be both father and mother unto me" (39). John saw to his younger brother's education. A new schoolmaster replaced the old one, who had died, and "it so fell out by God's good providence that this man stirred up in my heart a love and desire of the honor of learning, and therefore I told my friends I would be a scholar" (39). Shepard worked hard at his studies in Greek and Latin, took notes on the sermons he heard, and through the kind intercession of a Fellow of Emmanuel College in Cambridge was admitted to Emmanuel—where the Puritan influence was strong—at the age of fifteen.

In describing Shepard's years at Cambridge, John A. Albro astutely notes Luther's observation that three experiences are necessary to form a theologian: study, prayer, and temptation. Like St. Augustine, whose influence on the Reformation was immense, Shepard struggled with the sin and guilt he found inseparable from his own nature. Attending to the Word as preached by Laurence Chaderton and other ministers, Shepard was awakened to the terror of hell and the need for repentance. But his visions of eternity faded next to his love of "lust and pride and gaming and bowling and drinking" (41).

After becoming "dead drunk" one night, Shepard fled the following day to a field, where, brooding on his condition, he felt Christ's presence. Christ did not "justly . . . cut me off in the midst of my sin," Shepard emphasized, but "did meet me with much sadness of heart and troubled my soul for . . . my sins." When "I was worst," he says, "he began to be best unto me" (41). Yet despite the promptings of grace, through which Shepard resolved "to set upon a course of daily meditation," he remained unaware of the full depths of his "sinful nature" (41).

His real awareness, painful and experiential, emerged only through his conversion. Listening to a sermon by John Preston, an extremely influential Puritan preacher, Shepard was moved by the Word, now made effectual rather than merely rhetorical:

> the first sermon he preached was Romans 12—be renewed in the spirit of your mind—in opening which point, viz., the change of heart in a Christian, the Lord so bored my ears as that I understood what he spake and the secrets of my soul were laid upon [i.e., open] before me—the hypocrisy of all my good things I thought I had in me—as if one had told him of all that ever I did, of all the turnings and deceits of my heart,

insomuch as that I thought he was the most searching preacher in the world. (41–42)

Even after this dramatic moment, Shepard continued to be tormented by doubts over the existence of God, Christ's miracles, and his own salvation in light of his unworthiness and the threat of eternal reprobation. The anguish of his conflicts and struggles as he attempted to sustain his faith testifies to the nature of conversion as a beginning rather than as an accomplished certainty. As Jonathan Edwards wrote a century later, "when persons are converted they do but begin their work, and set out in the way they have to go."[5] Yet throughout this anguish, Shepard consistently refers to God's saving intervention in the act of conversion. He had even contemplated suicide during his years at Cambridge, he wrote, because his tormenting doubts reappeared "like beggars to my dore." But Christ interceded between the bridge and the water, he testified, and light banished darkness. Now, he asked rhetorically, "why shall I question that Truth which I have both known and seen?"[6]

So deep and intense was Shepard's experience of conversion that he resolved to become a Puritan minister, or priest. In 1623, Shepard had received his Cambridge B.A., and four years later he was awarded the M.A. On 12 July 1627 he was ordained a deacon in the Church of England and became a priest the following day. Sympathetic to the Puritan movement because of its strong presence at Cambridge in general and Emmanuel in particular, and deeply influenced by the preaching of John Preston and other Puritans, Shepard went to live in the home of Thomas Weld, vicar of Terling, Essex. Weld, with Thomas Hooker, who preached at Chelmsford, Essex, provided guidance for the newly ordained Shepard. Weld and Hooker both preceded Shepard in migrating to New England a few years later, where they became powerful forces in establishing and sustaining its Puritan structures and spirit. Their friendship and counsel, Shepard later recalled, helped his life and ministry immensely, for he was "so young and weak and unexperienced and unfit for so great a work" (47).

After some discussion with his fellow ministers concerning the nature and setting of his pastorate, Shepard decided to respond to the call of a congregation in Earles-Colne, a town in Essex. Decades after Shepard's death, according to later commentators, the people of Earles-Colne still recalled the young Shepard's intensely powerful preaching. But the years 1627 to 1630 were turbulent ones for the Church of England, and the power of Shepard's preaching, like that of other Puritan dissenters, ordained or not, reverberated through the established structures of the hierarchy. While he was preaching at Earles-Colne and later about to return to his home village of Towcester to become minister there, the high-church Anglican party accused Shepard of nonconformity and determined to silence his preaching and ministry.

During these years, Shepard insisted, he was committed wholly neither to the Puritan nor to the high-church position: "I was not resolved either way, but was dark in these things" (48). But Archbishop Laud, seeing in Puritan nonconformity the seeds of political and religious disorder, and sensing a threat in Shepard's Puritan connections and sympathies as well as in his preaching, summoned Shepard to London in December of 1630. In forbidding Shepard to preach or exercise any aspect of his ministry in the London diocese, Laude apparently had little patience with Shepard's protestations. In his *Autobiography,* Shepard argues that his preaching during this time centered on three elements: showing the people their misery; offering Christ as their remedy; and describing how they should respond to Christ's redemptive mercy. From Laud's perspective, however, the subversive political implications of the Puritan movement were ominous and demanded quelling. In recounting his confrontation with Laud, Shepard indicates how polarized the political and religious situation had become. Laud was, writes Shepard, "a fierce enemy to all righteousness and a man fitted of God to be a scourge to his people." After "many railing speeches against me," he "forbade me to preach, and not only so, but if I went to preach anywhere else his hand would reach me" (49).

Shepard's imagery of violence and warfare accurately reflects the intensity of the opposition between the Puritan movement and the established Anglican hierarchy symbolized by Laud and sanctioned by Charles I, who assumed the throne in 1625, five years before Shepard was silenced.[7] To the Puritans, Laud represented a complacent blending of aristocratic culture, conventional forms of worship rife with Roman Catholic "ornamentation," and a scandalous indifference to "experimental," or experiential, religious faith. But to the Anglican establishment, the Puritans seemed to desire a revolution against all hierarchical order, a rejection of church liturgy and tradition, and an embracing of personal faith at the expense of the corporate church and political and religious order. While the Puritans considered themselves to be saints, or believers, by the calling of God's grace, the hierarchy interpreted their vision as an invitation to disorder, schism, and heresy. Between Shepard and Laud in 1630, as between the established order and the vanguard of Puritan ministers calling for a reformation of ritual and spirit, there were few bridges. As the Anglican divine Richard Hooker had remarked, the Puritans insisted on the truth of their doctrine "although the world by receiving it be clean turned upside down."[8] Yet as Perry Miller notes, the truth by whose grace the Puritans believed themselves illumined may have been "foolishness and fanaticism" to those who opposed their vision and claim, but to the Puritans themselves "it was life eternal."[9]

Always moving under the shadow of Laud's condemnation, Shepard returned briefly to Towcester to preach. But finding no security in the town of his birth or in the wider region of Essex, Shepard responded to the call of a fellow minister, Ezekiel Rogers, who later joined Shepard in New England. Rogers encouraged Shepard to become chaplain to the family of Sir Richard Darley of Buttercrambe, Yorkshire. Alone, weary, and depressed, Shepard assumed his chaplaincy. In keeping with the dialectic of abandonment and redemption, alienation and restoration that typified his university days, the pattern of Shepard's life continued. He met in Darley's household Margaret Touteville, Darley's cousin, a woman "every way amiable and holy and endued with a very sweet spirit of prayer" (53). After a year's courtship, they were married on 23 July 1632. The presence of his "incomparably loving" wife signified that once again when Shepard's "adversaries intended most hurt to me, the Lord was then best unto me" (53).

The happiness of the newlywed couple was short-lived. Bishop Richard Neile, vigorously enforcing Laud's judgment on all dissenters and on Shepard in particular, ordered the local bishop of Durham, Thomas Morton, to prevent Shepard from preaching in Heddon, near Newcastle, to which Shepard had been called. Many of Shepard's Puritan friends in the ministry, including Thomas Weld, John Cotton, Thomas Hooker, and Samuel Stone, departed for New England amid these stages of persecution. Margaret, suffering through a difficult and near-fatal childbirth, gave birth to a son, Thomas. Fearful for their safety, convinced of the evil of the direction and rites of the current Anglican order, and seeing "the Lord departing from England when Mr. Hooker and Mr. Cotton were gone" and "the hearts of most of the godly set and bent" (55) toward New England's way, Shepard and his wife determined to sail for Boston.

In October 1634 Shepard, Margaret, and their son embarked from Harwich, in Essex, on a ship called the *Hope of Ipswich.* But the bitterly cold winter, rough weather, and high winds brought a harrowing time in which, writes Shepard, "the Lord's wonderful terror and mercy to us did appear" (57). Driven back by a storm, their ship ran onto the sands. Aware of the many other ships lost in the storm, and convinced that the winds and brutal weather had uprooted their remaining anchor, the crew "came to us and bid us look (pointing to the place) where our graves should shortly be" (59). Miraculously, however, all were saved: "a little rope held the cable, and the cable the little anchor, and the little anchor the great ship in this great storm" (60). Yet in the midst of their deliverance through God's mercy, says Shepard, their suffering continued. Their child, seized by illness, died, and was buried at Yarmouth. Shepard, fearful that he would be apprehended by vigilant church authorities, could not attend the burial, and describes this experience as an especially bitter affliction.

Returning to their friends in England, the Shepards lived in the town of Bastwick during the winter and then traveled to London, where, on 5 April 1635, their second son, also named Thomas, was born. Accompanied by Roger Harlakenden, John Wilson, Shepard's brother, Samuel, and other friends, Shepard and his family set sail once more for Boston in August 1635. Despite the violence of the storms and a precarious journey, they arrived safely in New England on 3 October. Margaret had fallen ill with tuberculosis during the voyage and later died. Yet the couple now rejoiced at their deliverance from their enemies and at their inclusion "among God's people, and also the child under God's precious ordinances" (64).

New England

Jonathan Mitchel, Shepard's successor in his pastorate at Newtown, later called Cambridge, described Shepard as a "Soul-melting Preacher."[10] Mitchel's evaluation of Shepard was typical. The very beginning of one of Shepard's most technical and difficult works suggests the cadenced clarity of his prose: "Time is one of the most precious blessings, which worthless man in this world enjoies, a jewel of inestimable worth, a golden stream dissolving, and as it were, continually running down by us, out of one eternity into another; yet seldom taken notice of untill it is quite passed away from us; Man (saith Solomon) knows not his time."[11]

Yet Shepard's rhetorical power as a preacher must always be viewed in light of his varied and dynamic ministry to church and society. He served as pastor at Cambridge until his death, and throughout his fourteen years there he journeyed with John Eliot and others among the Indian tribes of New England; contributed greatly to the founding of Harvard College and acted unofficially as its chaplain; defined and defended with energy and skill the Puritan vision in its doctrinal and pragmatic dimensions; and struggled with his family and culture through afflictions both intensely personal and seemingly apocalyptic. His life in New England embodies the Puritan search for the Kingdom of God and for the approximation of that Kingdom in time and space, while his relentless attempts to resolve the dilemmas and dualities that mark such a large part of the Puritan vision bear out the truth of Samuel Eliot Morison's observation that "life never came easy to Shepard, so exalted was the standard that he set for himself. Although reputed the most successful pastor of his day in leading lost souls to God, he was never satisfied."[12]

Our understanding of Shepard's intense commitment to his ministry was deepened by the publication in 1981 of *Thomas Shepard's Confessions,* or, as the manuscript is titled, *The Confessions of Diverse Propounded to be Received and Were Entertained as Members.* The work makes central the rigor of Shepard's standards for examining and admitting potential members to his Cambridge congregation in light of Puritan doctrine.[13] Shepard had been made pastor of this congregation of gathered Puritan believers, or "visible saints," shortly after his arrival at Cambridge. His transcriptions of the personal confessions of faith and conversion uttered by aspiring church members in front of the congregation reflect the intense drama of the Puritan religious experience. Yet whatever the degree of Shepard's stringency in light of the general standards for church membership in New England, the standards themselves were far more demanding than those set down by St. Augustine, the Roman Catholic church, Luther, or Calvin. It was part of the Puritan mission, wrote Shepard, to respond negatively to its own rhetorical question: "Can light and darknesse, Christ and Belial agree together" and "haters of all godlinesse and reformation, cleave together in one Church of Christ, with the Saints of God?"[14] As God's saints reformed and purified the old Anglican order in the New England wilderness, he insisted, it was their further task to bring into visible form and structure light and not darkness, Christ and not Satan, and God's faithful community of the elect rather than Satan's lukewarm legions.

In word and act, Shepard's devotion to these tasks was relentless. On specific doctrinal questions, he wrote such works as *The Church-Membership of Children, and Their Right to Batisme* and *Theses Sabbaticae, or the Doctrine of the Sabbath.* In 1648, the New England Puritans ratified the Cambridge Platform at a church synod in Cambridge. It was printed in 1649, the year of Shepard's death, and represented the most significant and inclusive statement of the doctrine and polity of what became known as nonseparating Congregationalism or the "New England Way." Although such ministers as Richard Mather and Thomas Hooker were instrumental in formulating this statement, Shepard's influence also pervaded its basic theological and eccelesiastical tenets. He also wrote a widely used catechism, *The First Principles of the Oracles of God,* and in *The Parable of the Ten Virgins,* a series of sermons he preached between 1636 and 1640, Shepard described in both terrifying and tender imagery the nature of God's convenant with the church on earth and with the besieged churches and "holy Nation" of New England which God had especially summoned.

Faithfulness to God's summons was the charge of Shepard's pastoral sermons and jeremiads from the very beginning, for Shepard envisioned the churches as under siege by Satanic forces of chaos and disbelief. Shepard's voyage from England had led him into a concretely turbulent rather than an ideal setting, and in the doctrinal and personal divisions and conflicts he encountered, he wrote, "the ancient and received truth came to be darkened, God's name was to be blasphemed, the churches' glory diminished, many godly grieved, many wretches hardened, deceiving and being deceived growing worse and worse" (*A*, 65). At the heart of this subversion of Puritan order was Antinomianism, Shepard insisted, and its primary exponent in New England, Anne Hutchinson.

A loyal follower of John Cotton and his preaching, Hutchinson emigrated to New England and came to personify for Shepard the radically subjective form of religious experience and rejection of earthly authority by which Antinomianism was marked. Shepard viewed Hutchinson and her followers as political and spiritual anarchists who constituted a lethal threat to New England's civil order as well as to its interpretation of the order of salvation. Many of Shepard's sermons addressed this dark and agonizing state of disorder within the Puritan experiment, and in 1637 and 1638 Shepard assumed a leading and energetic role in the church trial of Anne Hutchinson and her subsequent banishment from Massachusetts Bay.

In appealing to Scripture during Hutchinson's trial, Shepard implicitly and explicitly appeals to tradition as well, especially in light of Hutchinson's claim that inspiration comes to each believer by the direct infusion of the Holy Spirit and that such immediate and special revelations supersede all other sources of authority. To be sure, the Puritans valued experiential religion and piety. Yet they had strong ties to older forms and expressions of the Christian tradition. Indeed, in their battle against the Antinomians, the Puritans found themselves closer to certain late medieval Roman Catholic or Scholastic positions on the relationship between faith and works than to some Protestant reformers who rejected medieval scholasticism.

Since the forms of Protestant and Puritan piety had deep medieval roots, however, Shepard's knowledge of such Dominican thinkers as Thomas Aquinas and Franciscans as Duns Scotus, and his sympathy for aspects of their thought, is not surprising. The Puritan strain of piety, unlike some others, venerated learning and a learned ministry. As the Puritan faith sought a deeper understanding, it sanctioned all the disciplines of rhetoric, logic, philosophy, theology, and scientific investigation as means of illuminating further the natural world, man's self-understanding, and God's glory. In his own writings, Shepard's learning is unobtrusive yet obvious, and he freely cites the Jesuit theologian, Bellarmine, as frequently as he does Luther or Calvin. One of his first orders of business in helping to found Harvard College consisted in pleading with his friends in England to send him theological and philosophical works—especially those by the Scholastics—for the college library.

Whether Shepard was a close friend of John Harvard is not wholly clear, but it is certain that Shepard was a pivotal figure in planning for, founding, and nurturing Harvard College. He also petitioned successfully to institute scholarships for needy students. In light of their respect for learning and their need to educate the next generation and later ones for the vocation of the ministry and for other learned professions, the Puritans had determined to found a college. They chose Newtown, which they now called Cambridge in honor of the university where most of them had been educated, in large measure because Shepard had preserved his local congregation from the heresies of Antinomianism. His conception of the Puritan spirit as he envisioned its expression in visible Puritan churches and in their liturgical and doctrinal practices clearly represented to the larger Massachusetts Bay society the orthodoxy it desired to profess and defend.

Even as Shepard was preoccupied with the Antinomian controversy, his preaching and pastoral duties in his own congregation, his theological contributions to what would become the doctrine and polity of the Cambridge Platform, and his work in establishing Harvard College, he committed his time and energy to the American Indians. One commentator has argued that except for John Eliot, the apostle to the Indians, there was no one besides Shepard "to whom the Indians were more indebted for those measures which concerned their civil or their spiritual welfare."[15] Although the first missionary station in Cambridge, overseen by John Eliot, was not established until 1646, three years before Shepard's death, he traveled among the Indians in the years preceding and set in motion plans for assisting them through formal education, religious instruction, and other means. In 1655, Harvard founded an Indian College in order to educate Indian students, and while the project proved a failure, its initiation reflected Shepard's earlier labors.

Shepard wrote in whole or in part two works based on his experiences among the Indians: *The Day-Breaking, if not the Sun-Rising of the Gospell With the Indians in New-England* (1647) and *The Clear Sun-shine of the Gospel Breaking Forth upon the Indians in New-England* (1648). Although it is possible in retrospect to see in Shepard's tone and assumptions his sense of English superiority—Roger Williams seems to have been one of the very few Puritans who believed that the English could learn from the American Indians rather than the reverse—it is also necessary to acknowledge his desire to understand Indian beliefs and ways, his compassion, and his desire for moral and political justice. A given culture's assumption of superiority is hardly a phenomenon limited to the English or to the seventeenth century. Shepard's vision of the potential conversion of the Indians as part of a cosmic drama is an apocalyptic one rooted in the messianic fervor of New England Puritanism. But even in the light of the inevitable tendency of any culture to identify its form of civilization with God's own order and will, and to intermix its earthly predispositions with the Gospel, Shepard's work among the Indians was no pure imperialism. He identified with their humanity, prayed for their conversion as he did for the world's, and felt keenly the difficulties and failures inherent in the Puritan attempt to bring Indian customs into a form of harmony with English habits of mind, belief, and social expression. Under the aspect of eternity, Shepard consistently recalls, all human beings are made in God's image. A certain wonder at and respect for the existence and nature of the Indians' culture weaves its way through Shepard's works, and the human, personal, and fellow-creaturely dimension of his apocalyptic vision is persistently evident.

In the midst of his religious, political, and social activities, Shepard sought to sustain a fulfilling domestic life. Yet his family was afflicted by the sickness, suffering, and early deaths so pervasive in this time. Soon after arriving in New England, Margaret Shepard died of the tuberculosis she had contracted on the voyage. Their son, Thomas, was baptized after their arrival. Later seized by blindness, he recovered. In October 1637 Shepard married Joanna Hooker, the oldest daughter of Thomas Hooker. They were married for nine years and had three children: a boy who died "before he saw the sun, even in the very birth"; Samuel, who was born in 1641, became a respected and beloved minister at Rowley, and died at the age of twenty-seven; and John, who lived only four months. In giving birth to John, on 2 April 1646, Joanna died. On 8 September 1647 Shepard married for the third time, and he and his wife, Margaret Boradel, had a son, Jeremiah, born on 11 August 1648. After Shepard's death, Margaret married Jonathan Mitchel, who assumed Shepard's pastorate in the church at Cambridge.

The intensity of Shepard's recorded responses to the tragic events in his life, and to such anxieties as the stressful period when he fell into debt or the tensions generated by his future father-in-law Thomas Hooker's departure from Massachusetts Bay for a ministry in Connecticut, reflect the full depth of his humanity. In describing Joanna's death, Shepard recalls movingly that she had longed to die after the inner pain and suffering generated by the death of their first-born infant son. He questions the timing of her death and agonizes over the relationship between God's will and the death of a woman of such personal and spiritual beauty. Although scourged by affliction, he writes, "I am the Lord's, and he may do with me what he will. He did teach me to prize a little grace gained by a cross as a sufficient recompense for all outward losses. But this loss was very great" (70). Like Michael Wigglesworth, who lamented that "it is very hard for me to set my heart upon God himself and not to rest in the creature, or else to be restless and disconsolate," and like all other believers struggling with the demons of doubt and disbelief, Shepard felt deeply the conflicts heightened by his faith.[16] In seeking to resolve them, he consistently reveals his intensely human feelings. Joanna died praying for Christ's grace, and "the last sacrament before her lying in seemed to be full of Christ and thereby fitted for heaven." Further, Shepard knows that redemption can emerge from affliction. Yet the dialectic and tensions crystallized by Joanna's death continue: "Thus God hath visited and scourged me for my sins and sought to wean me from this world, but I have ever found it a difficult thing to profit even but a little by the sorest and sharpest afflictions" (71).

On 25 August 1649, Shepard died at the age of forty-four. He had suffered from a sore throat and the developing infection proved fatal. Even for a period, place, and people much given to hagiography and fervent eulogies, New England's lament over Shepard's death and praise for his life and devotions were striking. His voice had been a "silver trumpet" and he had preached the Gospel's salvific power with the efficacy of Augustine and Chrysostom. Shepard's spiritual strength shone through his physical weakness, wrote Edward Johnson in the *Wonder-Working Providence,* for he was a holy, "sweet-affecting, and soul-ravishing Minister" in whose soul "the Lord shed abroad his love so abundantly, that thousands of souls have cause to blesse God for him." He was, Johnson continued, "a man of a thousand," and each faithful and orthodox Puritan had reason to thank God for "Sending thee Shepard, safe through Seas awaie, / To feed his flock unto thy ending day." In his *Magnalia,* Cotton Mather's hagiography of Shepard echoed these encomiums and repeated two lines of a Latin elegy written by one of Shepard's friends. Its sentiments are representative of the common view: "His name and office sweetly did agree, / Shepard by name, and in his ministry."

Autobiography

In *The Sound Believer,* Shepard states that "the Lord's great plot is to gather all his elect under the wings of Christ" and to call them home "by the voice of the Gospel."[17] In his edition of the *Autobiography,* Michael McGiffert uses the phrase "God's plot" to describe Shepard's vision of the workings of divine grace and of God's incessant attempts to bring order out of chaos, light out of darkness, and individual redemption out of a personal state of abandonment and despair. The form of Shepard's *Autobiography* exemplifies the spiritual autobiography, conversion narrative, or confession. Its roots are to be found in Augustine's *Confessions* and in such narratives as John Bunyan's *Grace Abounding.* Above all, the *Autobiography* is an imaginative and dramatic story in which order and chaos, Christ and Satan, and grace and the powers of darkness contend for Shepard's soul and for the soul of the earthly church.

A medieval saint distinguished among three kinds of pilgrims, or wayfarers: those who leave their homeland in body but not in spirit; those who leave in spirit alone; and the most worthy, those who leave in body, spirit, and will. In his search for the Kingdom of God and in his desire to live *in patria,* in his true country, Shepard shows himself to be this third kind of wayfarer. His journey is at once inward in its self-reflectiveness, outward in its movement through a turbulent world, and supernatural in its dialectical relationship with a transcendent and saving God who repeatedly rescues Shepard through a convenant of grace. Further, it is always graphic and concrete, a corporeal as well as a spiritual journey. As he describes their deliverance from the violent storm that drove their ship onto the sands in their first embarkation from England, Shepard depicts an allegorical sense of terror and salvation that is simultaneously literal and spiritual. Their anchor had miraculously held the ship, writes Shepard, when someone "perceived that we were so strangely preserved" and said, "That thread we hang by will save us, for so we accounted of the rope fastened to the anchor, in comparison of the fierce storm." And so it did save them, Shepard continues, "the Lord showing his dreadful power toward us and yet his unspeakable rich mercy to us who in depths of mercy heard, nay helped, us where we could not cry through the disconsolate fears we had out of these depths of seas and miseries. This deliverance was so great that I then did think if ever the Lord did bring me to shore again I should live like one come and risen from the dead" (60).

In this vivid and even apocalyptic passage, Shepard identifies their actual near-shipwreck with the storms, afflictions, and darkness of life, and their deliverance with the intervention of divine grace. In his later sermons, he repeatedly returns to this nautical imagery, with its deeply biblical echoes: the anchor of faith, the danger of spiritual shipwreck, and the prototypical image of conversion, the Israelites' crossing of the Red Sea in their Exodus from death to new life. In their merging of physical experience and allegorical meaning, events become for Shepard signs or "types" of God's ongoing revelation in the natural world. One of the sailors falls into the sea but is "supported by a divine hand." As the sailor recovers from an apparently certain death, Shepard assents to the view of a "godly man" in the ship that "This man's danger and deliverance is a type of ours, for he did fear dangers were near unto us, and that yet the Lord's power should be shown in saving of us" (58).

As a narrative of deliverance, Shepard's dramatic account and interpretation of his own journey from darkness to light, and that of his fellow believers, emphasizes three major images and themes: the world and the wayfaring soul as battlegrounds over which God and Satan, order and chaos, perpetually move and contend for dominance; the crucial role of conversion, and of grace and faith, in providing what Augustine called "a place to stand" in the midst of darkness and affliction; and the mystery of redemption in Christ, both individual and communal, as it rises out of the most intense suffering and despair. Shepard's prose style is graphic and intense. As it dramatizes these themes, it seeks to witness to God's sovereign power and saving grace as well as to Shepard's faith, anxiety, and gratitude. It also points to the overarching importance of memory and retrospection as the only means by which experience may be truly confronted and clearly known. Only long after their Exodus do the Israelites look back on it, comprehend its meaning, and witness to its wonder by writing it as testament for themselves and for others. Only in the last three years of his life does Shepard do the same for his own, and the New England Puritans', deliverance. For him memory can be, and here is, redemptive.

That memory and the sharing and transmitting of his story are at the heart of Shepard's vision is evident from his addressing his manuscript to his son, "so that he may learn to know and love the great and most high God, the God of his father." Although his son was not yet born when they left for New England, Shepard tells him, "yet thou wert in the dangers of the sea in thy mother's womb then, and see how God hath miraculously preserved thee, that thou art still alive and thy mother's womb and the terrible seas have not been thy grave. Wonder at and love this God forever" (33). Just as the Lord had brought Shepard "to shore again" as "one come and risen from the dead," so his son has been resurrected through God's gracious covenant.

In light of Shepard's imagery and typology as they represent his interpretation of the world and his own experience, especially before his conversion, these consistent references to redemption and resurrection are even more dramatic. For Shepard describes his life as fragmented, restless, and despairing. Our heart is restless, wrote Augustine, until it rest in God; yet for Shepard, as for the searching Augustine, peace and rest are nowhere to be found. Further, his experiences lead him to states of confusion and anxiety that become forms of a living death. The town to which he is sent to escape the plague is "most blind" (38). The world is cruel, his parents are dead, and his disposition is that of a "heartlessness to any good and loathing of God's ways" (44). In a world of political, religious, and personal fragmentation, Shepard is without identity.

Although he sensed his sinfulness and hated his excesses of drinking, wastefulness, and self-pity, states Shepard, he was not fully aware of the depth of his alienation from the God he was unconsciously seeking. Only through his conversion on hearing and genuinely experiencing St. Paul's words in Romans during John Preston's sermon did Shepard begin to know his own condition. For Augustine, as now for Shepard, the flux and immediacy of moments of time resist interpretation and meaning. Only in finding a place to stand, a vantage point of stability, can we observe ourselves clearly, and only through conversion can we discover such a place and perspective. Without such a perspective, there can be no judgment and understanding of the "old self," the "self that was," by the "new self," the "self that is." But though the miraculous act of conversion, both past and present can be viewed under the aspect of eternity as self-identity is located and what was lost becomes found. Christ is at once anchor, foothold, and perspective.

Yet in the aftermath of this experience of conversion, Shepard's anxieties and doubts intensified and his condition reflected Wigglesworth's lament: "Fearful shakings frequently assail me, and I would stand fast upon the word of God but I can find no foothold."[18] Doubting his own election by God's grace and questioning both Christ's authority and miracles, Shepard feared that he had committed the unpardonable sin of absolute despair. He contemplated suicide and felt "the terrors of God . . . break in like floods of fire into my soul." He was convinced that God in his wrath had cast him away among the damned rather than embracing him as one of the elect: "I did see God like a consuming fire and an everlasting burning, and myself like a poor prisoner leading to that fire, and the thought of eternal reprobation and torment did amaze my spirits" (43).

In this relentless onslaught of fear and doubt, however, the seemingly perennial presence of grace makes itself felt in Shepard's heart. Luther had been terrified above all by his vision of God's absolute righteousness, or *justitia,* which condemned him as unworthy and consigned him to be eternally lost. Yet through God's grace and through faith alone—*justitia sola fidei*—he came to see that God's righteousness meant not anger and condemnation but a promise of mercy. In the same way, Shepard's agonizing introspection consistently sees mercy and grace in a dialectical relationship with his terror of judgment and with his own despair. As Christ comes to him, "the terrors of the Lord began to assuage sweetly" (44). In reflecting on Christ as his sole Redeemer, and on his own sinfulness as a way of recognizing his need for Christ rather than his irrevocably lost state, "I was kept from sinkings of heart and did beat Satan as it were with his own weapons" (45).

Although Shepard notes that his turbulent conflicts and his experiences of grace antedated his encounter with Preston and other preachers—"I saw Christ teaching me this before any man preached any such thing unto me," he writes—he consistently returns to the mediation of Scripture and the act of preaching as the instruments of his conversion and his attentiveness to Christ. After despairingly recognizing that "I had no assurance Christ was mine," Shepard listens once more to one of Preston's sermons. As Preston explains, or "opens" a text from 1 Corinthians on Christ's wisdom and redemption, Shepard began "to prize him and he became very sweet unto me." He had known intellectually of the importance of receiving the offered Christ "as Lord and Savior and Husband," he writes, but his will rebelled: "I found my heart ever unwilling to accept of Christ upon these terms; I found them impossible for me to keep that condition, and Christ was not so sweet as my lust. But now the Lord made himself sweet to me and to embrace him and to give up myself unto him" (45).

In his use of marital and love imagery, Shepard dramatizes God's covenant of grace as it persistently offers itself to the wayward soul. Despite the fears and doubts that followed this experience, Shepard comes to a real sense of Christ's free mercy, "and here I did rest" (45). The verb "rest" echoes Augustine's *Confessions* as well as a description of faith common to the Puritans: a "resting of the heart in God." Even Shepard's further anxiety over whether Christ's righteousness "for a poor sinner's ungodliness" would be given and applied specifically to him leads to comfort in this setting. Once more, Scripture and Christ constitute the dominant images of salvation: "The Lord made me see that so many as receive him, he gives power to be the sons of God (John 1:12), and I saw the Lord gave me a heart to receive Christ with a naked hand, even naked Christ, and so the Lord gave me peace" (45–46).

Cotton Mather described Shepard's life as "a trembling walk with God." In the *Autobiography,* and to a still greater extent in the meditations of his *Journal,* the intensity of Shepard's awe and trembling before God's holiness and his own fallen state is consistently striking. The dialectic between his sin and God's deliverance, his gratitude and relapses, repentance and failure, is ongoing. When he thanks God for the wondrous experience of meeting and marrying his first wife, Margaret, he accounts it a gift "for which mercy to me in my exiled condition in a strange place I did promise the Lord that this mercy should knit my heart the nearer to him and that his love should constrain me." But, he continues, "I have ill requited the Lord since that time and forgot myself and my promise also" (53).

Yet Shepard's retrospective understanding of the pattern of his experience as providential rests on his conviction that divine grace is constant and irresistible. After his conversion, he noted, he was never tempted to accept Arminianism, a theological position that professed among other doctrines the freedom of the will, precisely because his own experience "so sensibly" confuted it. The workings of his natural will led him into confusion and darkness; only a supernatural grace redeemed it, and Shepard, from a permanent state of loss and abandonment. The often-agonizing oppositions between nature and grace, sin and election, despair and assurance, the temptation "to serve Satan without promise, to foresake the Lord against promise" (76), and many other conflicts and tensions of a dramatically binary nature mark Shepard's *Autobiography* as surely as they mark the Puritan mind and imagination. Shepard's attempts to resolve them center on the same mystery as Kierkegaard's attempts two centuries later to make compatible the "inheritance" of original sin and the "ethical and spiritual" dimension of guilt. How can reason link a natural and biological category to a spiritual one?, Kierkegaard wonders; then he responds to his own bewilderment: "It must be believed. The paradox in Christian truth is invariably due to the fact that it is truth as it exists for God. The standard of measure and the end is superhuman; and there is only one relationship possible: faith."[19]

For Shepard, the earthly and ultimate promises and pitfalls to which religious experience in general and the Puritan movement in particular are attentive are communal as well as personal. A radically individualistic strain certainly constitutes one dimension of Puritanism. Yet only a few years after Shepard's death, his compatriot Wigglesworth defined himself in relation to a larger community in a way also typical of Shepard when he wrote in his *Diary,* "gods gradual departure from my self, and from this whole country . . . took deep impression on me."[20] Shepard's vision also incorporates this consistently social and apocalyptic aspect. The individual soul, the soul of the church in New England, and, ultimately, the soul of America itself are indissolubly joined for good or evil. The Lord, writes Shepard, is "the God that brought me out of Egypt, that profane and wicked town where I was born" (72). Yet his Egyptian bondage is also that of the Puritans, and his Red Sea, the Atlantic ocean, is also theirs, as are their communal wilderness, Promised Land, wayfaring, and destination.[21] The typology of these new Isaraelites, proclaiming and witnessing to the New Covenant, is individual and experiential yet magnified and shared.

Even in the most deeply introspective parts of the *Autobiography,* Shepard is aware of the presence of others, including John Preston, Thomas Hooker, and, of course, his wives, both as instruments in the process of his conversion and sanctification and as fellow creatures to whom he owes much and toward whom he feels gratitude and love. Their lives form exemplary patterns of faith and character. When Shepard expresses his fervent hope that God will "keep this poor church spotless and clear" (65) from heresy, corruption, and despair, he indicates that the communal and personal dimensions of his vision and aspirations are interwoven. Shepard's "heart is knit" to the church and its saints, and those who embody Satan's forces of darkness and oppression simply serve to intensify the enduring ties that bind Shepard to his fellow believers. Further, his own deliverance from darkness to light is potentially that of each wayfaring soul and all gathered believers as a whole. It is appropriate that he cites Augustine in the manuscript of his *Autobiography,* since the work itself, like all of Shepard's writing and preaching, shares the motive and end to which Augustine attributes the writing of his *Confessions:* "This is the fruit of my confessions of what I am, not of what I have been, to confess this, not before Thee only, in a secret exultation with trembling, and a secret sorrow with hope; but in the ears also of the believing . . . sharers of my joy, and partners in my mortality, my fellow-citizens, and fellow-pilgrims, who are gone before, or are to follow on, companions of my way."[22]

Chapter Two

Scripture and Sermon: The "Best Rhetorick" and the Voice of Salvation

The absolute and unique truth of the biblical word, says Ernst Cassirer, is the central doctrine for all schools of Reformation thought. In its transcendence, supernatural origin, and absolute authority, it constitutes the basis for the promise of salvation in Christ and the vehicle for the voice of the Holy Spirit. Through its primacy, "the religious individualism of the Reformation remains throughout oriented and confined to purely objective, supernaturally binding realities."[1] The Book of Scripture, as Jonathan Edwards often states, is the interpreter of the Book of Nature. Further, by God's spoken word light appears at the Creation; by exalting every word spoken by the mouth of God, Christ refutes the Devil during the temptation in the wilderness; and in the sacred words of the Law in the Old Testament as well as in Christ, the Word made flesh, the mystery and power of the word are made visible. In its light, all human speech had to be seen as referential and as reflecting its divine ground and end. The literal word, spoken or written, insists Shepard, is a dynamic mystery, and the knowledge and art of rhetoric must remain linked to the divine voice and its claims of eternal truth. Ultimately, he asks, "hath not Christ used the best rhetorick to winne us?"[2]

St. Augustine and the Reformation

For Calvin, Augustine is "the theologian." Luther was an Augustinian monk. Cassirer notes that the Protestant emphasis during the Reformation on the close relationship between the Word of God and the state of fallen man depends for its strength on the Augustinian conception of dogma. In his seminal *The New England Mind: The Seventeenth Century,* Perry Miller argues that "the Augustinian strain of piety" constitutes a fundamental part of the Puritan mind and spirit. For Shepard, as for the Puritans in general, Calvin, and Luther, Augustine remains the crucial patristic voice and influence. His name, experiences, and teachings echo throughout their letters, sermons, and treatises. The Protestant thought, doctrine, and spirit of which Puritanism is one expression continued to be consciously indebted to its Augustinian sources.

The Canons of the Synod of Dort (1619) embody the basic Calvinist doctrines to which the broad Puritan movement subscribed. They emphasized the absolute sovereignty of God, the authority of Scripture as the normative rule of faith and practice, a "limited atonement" in which Christ died not for universal salvation but for the salvation of a remnant of believers, or "elect," and the irresistible nature of grace. In following Luther and Calvin's stress on the bondage of man's intellect to error and his will to sin, the Calvinists adhered to the description of "natural man" in the Geneva Confession of 1536—a description they viewed as profoundly Augustinian: "We acknowledge man by nature to be blind, darkened in understanding, and full of corruption and perversity of heart, so that of himself he has no power to be able to comprehend the true knowledge of God . . . nor to apply himself to good works." Since man is hopelessly lost and fallen, "he has need to be illumined by God, so that he comes to the right knowledge of his salvation, and thus to be redirected in his affections and reformed to the obedience of the righteousness of God."[3]

The states of sin, abandonment, illumination and conversion, and perseverance are as central to Augustine's experience and *Confessions* as they are to the Geneva Confession, the Canons of Dort, and the Puritan creeds. Further, these descriptions of the human condition in its need for illuminating grace are rooted in the affirmation of the importance of the Word, and of words, in the process of salvation. Creeds themselves and other formal confessions of faith presuppose that language is a profession, a witness. Before the Holy Spirit becomes Shepard's voice of salvation through the preaching and hearing of the Word, he "took out a little book I have every day into the fields and writ down what God taught me lest I should forget . . . and so the Lord encouraged me and I grew much" (*A*, 42). Earlier, he names as one of his most anguished schoolboy memories his failure to take good and sufficient notes on the sermons he hears (*A*, 39). It is telling that the Puritans often refer to Augustine's conversion through his hearing and reading of the Word and that they appeal to his analysis of the potentially sacred or demonic use of words through rhetoric.

Augustine surely would assent to Shepard's argument that Christ's is the "best rhetorick." As with the entire series of oppositions so common to the Augustinian and Puritan visions, however, there is a "worst rhetoric" to counter the best just as evil seeks to counter goodness and Satan to counter Christ. The "unholy loves" Augustine hears singing to him include a love of rhetoric divorced from the eternal truth that alone gives words their deepest and most vital meaning. In his *Confessions,* as in his treatise *On Christian Doctrine,* Augustine consistently contrasts the empty words of the sophists and rhetoricians who lack faith to the salvific and holy words of those who, like St. Ambrose, faithfully preach the truth. By degrees, says Augustine, he came to care less about Ambrose's rhetorical eloquence and more about the substance of his words as he listened to his sermons: "together with the words . . . came also into my mind the things . . . for I could not separate them. And while I opened my heart to admit 'how eloquently he spake,' there also entered 'how truly he spake.' "[4]

Augustine's repudiation of eloquence without substance and his embracing of "the truth within words" ultimately comes about through the intercession of the Word spoken to him through Scripture. Although he is affected by hearing the stories of the conversion of Victorinus and the commitment of St. Antony, Augustine continues to suffer from the "two conflicting wills"[5] within him. His will to believe contends with the spirit of disbelief until, in the deepest affliction, he hears a voice, "as of boy or girl, I know not, chanting, and oft repeating, 'Take up and read; Take up and read.' " Taking the voice to be God's command to open the Scripture before him, and recalling Antony's conversion through hearing the Gospel preached, Augustine seizes the Book and reads St. Paul's exhortation to reject the spirit of disbelief and self-indulgence, or "the flesh," and to "put ye on the Lord Jesus Christ." Says Augustine: "No further would I read; nor needed I: for instantly at the end of this sentence, by a light as it were of serenity infused into my heart, all the darkness of doubt vanished away."[6]

For Luther, Jonathan Edwards, and Charles and John Wesley, among many others, a similar pattern of conversion centered on the voice of salvation through the Word constitutes the heart of their religious transformation, just as it had earlier for Antony, and, indeed, St. Francis. As a struggling Augustinian monk, Luther in his conversion both dramatizes and epitomizes the form and substance of their experiences. He wanted to believe in God's love and mercy, Luther writes, but he had come to visualize God and Christ only as terrifying judges. A single word in Paul's Epistle to the Romans, *justitia,* or God's "righteousness," embodied for Luther the personal anguish engendered by his fear of God's righteous wrath. But when he finally understood Paul's meaning—that God was merciful and will justify the true believer through faith and grace—he was transformed: "I felt that I was altogether born again and had entered Paradise through open gates. I extolled my sweetest word with a love as great as the hatred with which I had before hated the word 'righteousness of God.' Thus that place in Paul was for me truly the gate to Paradise."[7]

In this light, the Puritan insistence that Scripture is the primary voice through which the Holy Spirit summons the individual to salvation takes on a real sense of urgency. The structure and essence of the church, the rite of baptism, and the celebration of the sacrament of the Lord's Supper remain for the Puritans crucial and persistent concerns. Yet Puritan doctrine and the Puritan imagination root themselves firmly and deeply in the seminal and persistent efficacy of the voice of God speaking through Scripture. This emphasis entails for the Puritan movement and for Shepard, in his *Of Ineffectual Hearing the Word* and in his sermons and treatises as a whole, three major themes: the vital place of the sermon and its indispensable basis, a specific biblical text; the need for an understanding of Scripture, and a use of rhetoric, which respects the plain and literal sense or dimension of words; and the importance of moving the listener's will, or affections, rather than appealing to reason alone, in seeking a genuine experience of conversion.

As Douglas Bush and more recent commentators have emphasized, it is difficult to exaggerate the significance of the sermon in the seventeenth century. As Bush notes, "while the sermon had the unique character of a divine message, and carried the obligation of close scrutiny of the inspired text, it was also a highly developed literary form, the product of an unbroken oratorical tradition which went back to the ancients."[8] For the Puritans, the structure of the sermon is tripartite. By starting with the "opening," or exposition, of a particular biblical text, it points to the witness of the Holy Spirit through Scripture as the voice of revelation and salvation. By proceeding to the "doctrines" or "reasons" drawn from and informing the deepest meanings and implications of the opening of the biblical text, the sermon appeals to the intellectual understanding of the listener. And by concluding with an "application" or series of "uses," it addresses the will, or heart, or affections in its attempt to make the urgency of its message immediate and concrete rather than abstract and speculative. As figures as separated in time as Augustine and Edwards insisted, true religion cannot be practiced without engaging the affections.

The formal and rhetorical conventions of the Puritan sermon allowed for diverse styles. William Perkins, Richard Baxter, Thomas Adams, and John Preston share a common vision and a general style. Yet each of their styles expresses a distinctive voice. What they persistently share is a conviction that the sermon's language ought to be plain and clear. As John Downame argues in *The Christian Warfare,* "whereas men in their writings affect the praise of flowing eloquence and loftiness of phrase, the holy Ghost . . . hath used great simplicite and wonderfull plainesse, applying himselfe to the capacitie of the most unlearned."[9] Thomas Hooker also insists on the importance of "plainesse and perspicuity, both for matter and manner of expression," and he, like Downame, assents fully to Luther's description of the "style" of the Holy Spirit as the source and analogue of the best rhetorical style: "The Holy Spirit is the plainest writer and speaker in heaven and earth, and therefore His words cannot have more than one, and that the very simplest, sense, which we call the literal, ordinary, natural, sense."[10]

It is a rule, writes Shepard, "never to flie to metaphors, where there can be a plain sense given."[11] Although Augustine's interest in allegory and in the fourfold interpretation of Scripture may seem antithetical to this emphasis on the plain and literal dimension of scriptural and rhetorical language, he, like Thomas Aquinas, sought to anchor all allegory to its literal foundation. Perkins's famous assertion that a "wooden key" is better than a jeweled one in opening the mind and heart is in fact a direct and resonating echo of Augustine's admonition to those preoccupied with ornament and eloquence at the expense of truth: "Of what use is a gold key if it will not open what we wish? Or what objection is there to a wooden one which will, when we seek nothing except to open what is closed?"[12]

Although the complexities surrounding Puritan rhetoric, allegory, and biblical interpretation are many and varied, it is clear that the Puritans found in the plain and compelling voice of Scripture the most basic source and analogue for their own voice and style. Divorced from Scripture and faith, rhetoric could be demonic. Linked to them, it could assist the work of salvation. As Tertullian, the patristic thinker greatly influential in the seventeenth century, had argued, words are not only figures of speech but literal statements; they are bodies as well as shadows. He insists that "it was not figuratively that the Virgin conceived in her womb; nor in a trope did she bear Emmanuel, that is, Jesus, God with us." Ultimately, he concludes, "the realities are involved in the words, just as the words are read in the realities."[13]

The real purpose of rhetoric, writes Francis Bacon, is "to apply reason to imagination for the better moving of the will."[14] The vividness and energy of Tertullian's language clearly demonstrate that his goal is not simply to explain but to exhort and persuade. The ultimate end of preaching, Augustine insists, is to move adverse minds to conversion, and such movement must occur in the heart or affections. The light by which Augustine himself is transformed is "infused into [his] heart." If human beings were angels or creatures of pure reason, the Puritans often noted, they could be converted by logic alone. But humanity's fallen and sinful nature cannot be changed by axioms. Real conversion necessitates not only reason but imagination, not only logic but "a sense of the heart," and not only doctrinal principles but the illuminating and animating word of grace and faith.

The Promise of Conversion and *The Ineffectual Hearing of the Word*

In 1652, three years after Shepard's death, his *Treatise of Ineffectual Hearing the Word* was published in a single volume together with a longer work, *Subjection to Christ.*[15] In a preface, William Greenhill and Samuel Mather celebrated Shepard's memory by noting the "precious and deep remembrance" in which his former parishoners in England continued to hold him. Shepard preached each lecture-sermon in 1641. As is so often true of Shepard's writings, their publication came about not through Shepard's own fully prepared manuscripts but through the transcribed notes taken by his listeners. But while the form of the notes cannot capture precisely the manner of Shepard's real style, Greenhill and Mather tell us, it does capture its essence: "These notes may well be thought to be lesse accurate, then if the Author himself had published them, and to want some polishments and trimmings, which it were not fit for any other to adde; however thou wilt finde them full of useful truths, and mayest easily discern his Spirit, and a Spirit above his own breathing in them."

This animating spirit, they note, pervades Shepard's language. His manner of preaching was "close and searching, and with abundance of affection and compassion to his hearers." Shepard's style persistently aimed at a transparent clarity: "He affected plainesse together with power in preaching, not seeking abstrusities, nor liking to hover and soare aloft in dark expressions, and so to shoot his arrowes (as many Preachers do) over the heads of his hearers." Although some may argue that Shepard's sermons are somewhat "strict" or "legal," states the preface, the times have no need of "meal-mouth'd Preachers" and "toothless words." On the contrary: where there are no efficacious "Law-Sermons, there will be few Gospel-lives." Only a conscience awakened through hearing the law and Gospel preached can be attentive to God's voice. Yet, the preface concludes, "as there is much preaching, but few serious, few heart-breaking Sermons: so there is much hearing, but little effectual hearing."

This sharp distinction between the effectual, or true hearing of the word, and an ineffectual, or false hearing, underlies and informs the structure and substance of *Ineffectual Hearing.* Typically, Greenhill and Mather, like the Puritan mind and the religious movements of the seventeenth century in general, presuppose the crucial role of the sermon in the promise and work of conversion. Through every sermon we hear, Thomas Hooker remarks, each of us "is thereby nearer either to heaven or hell" and either "made better or worse by it."[16] Shepard's text in *Ineffectual Hearing* is John 5:37: "Ye have neither heard his voice at any time, nor seen his shape." Yet always present in the sermon, explicitly or implicitly, is Paul's insistence that "faith is by hearing, and hearing by the worde of God" (Rom. 10:17; *GB*). So central is this doctrine to Shepard's purposes that his description of the four ways, or testimonies, through which Christ's divine status as the Messiah is made known begins with John's testimony and that provided by Christ's works. But they conclude with two further spoken witnesses: the heavenly voice of the Father and "the voice of the Scriptures, the highest of all, and surer than a voice from heaven" (155).

As Shepard describes and interprets the nature of this voice of salvation and the ways in which the listener responds—or fails to respond—to its call, he emphasizes three major themes: the "twofold" aspect of the word and of all human responses to it, whether "notional" or "experiential"; the tension inherent in the soul's apprehension of the dialectical relationship between God's judgment and mercy, wrath and love, and its own fear of abandonment and hope of being found; and the peace and reassurance brought to God's chosen people, or elect, by Christ's voice and love.

Throughout *Ineffectual Hearing*, Shepard dwells on the many aspects of the double or twofold nature of hearing and knowledge. The "inward word is double" (158) in its division into an effectual and ineffectual form. Christians may be distinguished as may "two golden vessels" (179), one filled with grace and the other partially filled but longing for more sustenance. The word has "a double efficacy" (181) just as there are "two degrees of true knowledge of God in this life" (155). Informed by a strong sense of duality grounded in the Puritan conception of Scripture, logic, and salvation, Shepard sets the tone of his sermon by emphasizing the crucial distinction between actual and abstract hearing: "There is a twofold word, or rather a double declaration of the same word. 1. There is Gods external or outward word, containing letters and syllables, and this is his external voice. 2. There is Gods internal word and voice, which secretly speaks to the heart, even by the external word, when that only speaks to the eare" (157). Some heard Christ's parables, says Shepard, but because they did not hear truly Christ's words remained abstract sounds: "As 'tis with a painted Sun on the wall, you see the Sun and Stars, but there is a difference between seeing this and the Sun and Starres themselves, wherein is an admirable glory: go to a painted Sun, it gives you no heat, nor cherisheth you not; so it is here" (157).

Shepard's persistent descriptions of the chasm between an abstract or "notional" hearing and a response that is real and experiential reflect the Puritan insistence on the "affective" dimension of conversion. True conversion entails a sense of the heart. The Spirit, writes Calvin, "must penetrate into our hearts" in the form of a sensus, or "a conviction that requires no reasons" and "a knowledge with which the best reason agrees—in which the mind truly reposes more securely and constantly than in any reasons." This experience, he concludes, "can be born only of heavenly revelation."[17] Without this experiential gift, argues Shepard, the Word remains silent and the words of any preacher or sermon are but "the blowing of the winde upon a rock, which blusters for a time; but when the winde is down they are still" (161). In such a state, the condition of all unhearing souls is dreadful:

> One would wonder to see, that such things which a gracious heart thinks, this would draw every heart, yet [they] remaine not stir'd, things which the devils tremble at, and others which Angels wonder at, yet they hear not. Oh they hear not God speak, they are dead in their graves, farre from God; and there they are kept by the mighty powers of Satan, like one in a deep dark cave, kept by fiery dragons under the ground, and the tombstone is laid upon them. (161)

This apocalyptic description indicates how closely related are Shepard's conceptions of hearing and of the last things—death, judgment, heaven, and hell. The contrast between those who hear and those who remain deaf includes the contrast between God and Satan, angels and devils, and the ascending power of grace and oppressive gravity of death. Shepard's images are persistently opposed to each other in sharply dichotomous ways. In a literal, allegorical, and experiential sense, the believing soul seeks to mediate these contrasting forces. Nowhere is the drama of this struggle more pronounced than in the soul's existential awareness of God's judgment and love and its own fear and hope.

Grounded in conflict and a sense of incompleteness, the believer experiences "that great distance and infinite separation of mens soule from God" (160). Yet even in a state of blindness, despair, and fear of God's judgment, insists Shepard, a believer may have "such a glimpse (in hearing the word) of Gods grace . . . and the love of God to him, that he may be in a little heaven at that time; ravished in the admiration of that mercy, that ever God should look to him" (177). Echoing the Psalmist's astonishment that God should be mindful of man as well as the traditional experience of the convert who comes to recognize that God's mercy is identical to his justice, Shepard invokes the imagery of dryness and fertility to describe the process of conversion and assurance: "many times a Christian hath his flourishing time as the grasse, but when the grasse is mowen, it is as a dry chip; so the soul it may grow dry. . . . Now where is your sap and savour? but I tell you, if you belong to the Lord Jesus, the raine it will fall again . . . as the raine on the mowen grasse, and you know that it recovers little by little, and puts on a green coat again" (186).

In a quintessentially Puritan way, however, Shepard always remains mindful of the "everlasting conflict and warfare" (184) of the soul's struggle toward salvation. The soul "may have some such feare, reformation, affection, as may continue, but never carry him out of himself unto Christ" (171). Further, even when the soul is aware of God's attentiveness, danger abounds: "It is so, and the word sayes so, and the soul is ravished with wonderment" at God's mercy; "yet God is gone again, and the soul loses it" (177). For the Church Fathers and for the Scholastics, the pain of hell is the pain of loss, and for Shepard this suffering and anguish is a persistent and indispensable part of the experience of redemption.

In emphasizing throughout his sermon the profound difference between ineffectual and effectual hearing, Shepard consistently points to Christ as the mediator whose presence is the indispensable element in the work of salvation. Every aspect of God's word reflects Christ's atonement for man's sinfulness: "This blessed word and voice of God, every title of it cost the blood of Christ; written all the lines of it in the blood of Christ" (192–93). Man's heavenly and earthly happiness is to "close," or unite, with Christ. Christ is a healing sun, a kindler of faith and virtue, and a divine voice who opens the otherwise sealed book of Scripture. In a striking passage, Shepard uses the dialectic of terror and hope, judgment and love, to stress Christ's central place: "let the word speak what it will, whether terrour; Oh my need of Christ! mercy and grace; oh the love of Christ! oh the blood of Christ! Command; Oh that I may live to honour Christ, and wrong him no more! Duties; Oh the easie yoke of Christ! They look upon the whole Word rightly dispensed as the Bridegrooms voice, and truly his words are sweet" (171). Before his conversion, Luther said, he could envision Christ only as a stern and demanding judge who served to extend the wrath of the Father. But afterward, he came to experience Christ as perfect love and mercy. Here too in Shepard, Christ exists for the believer in a tension between judgment and mercy. Yet Shepard's concluding biblical image of Christ as a bridegroom speaking sweet words emphasizes Christ's solicitous love as his most powerful attribute.

Shepard also makes clear, however, that while Christ extends this love potentially to all, only the remnant, or elect, experience it in a saving or effectual way. For the Puritans, as for the Calvinists at the Synod of Dort, Christ's atonement was limited rather than universal in its application. Just as God perpetually saved the remnant of Israel rather than all of Israel's children and just as Christ's parables reached only those with eyes to see and ears to hear their deepest message, so God's "electing love" (193) is known only by those who are part of a chosen remnant. In rejecting the Arminian doctrine of universal atonement and salvation at the Synod of Dort, the traditional Calvinists embraced the doctrine of election, and the Puritans in general and Shepard in particular continued to subscribe to it. God's voice, he states, "none but the Elect hear" (158). In support of his position, Shepard cites the Epistle to the Romans: "the elect hathe obteined [grace], and the rest have bene hardened, According as it is written, God hathe given them the spirit of slomber: eyes that they shulde not se, and eares that they shulde not heare unto this day" (Rom. 7:7–8; *GB*).

For these unregenerate who cannot hear, God's voice remains silent: "they have indeed the Scriptures, and the precious Word of God dispensed to them; but the Lord never speaks one word unto them" (163). Many do not wish to have their reason illumined and their hearts moved: "a fat heart and an heavy eare ever go together" (165). Others listen to general principles but do not apply them to their own condition: "a man hears things generally delivered, the blessed estate of the Saints, the cursed estate of the wicked, consolations to the one, curses to the other, exhoratations to faith and obedience, to both, and a man sits by, and never thinks the Lord is speaking, and means me" (166). Even the very act of attending a sermon may spring from radically varying motives, insists Shepard: "When a man comes to hear a Sermon, there is a Sermon and the Market, there is a Sermon and a friend to speak withall; and so many young people will go abroad to hear Sermons; What is the end of it? It is, that ye may get wives and husbands many of you; but it is not your blessednesse to close with the Lord in his word" (191). The salvation of the elect is marked by their "closing" with Christ. But as the Puritan Samuel Ward emphasizes, "The non-elect never come to be justified by a true and lively faith, nor ever are by that bond mystically united to Christ as their seed, nor ever attain unto true repentance."[18] This contrast between the saved and the reprobate, between those who hear truly and those who remain deaf, remains at the heart of the Puritan assessment of the human condition and the movement of history.

Polarites: The Two Kingdoms

The intensity of the Puritan vision of salvation and history is generated in part by the persistent Puritan awareness of the polarities inherent in every form of ordinary and sacred experience. The dramatic conflicts between God and Satan, the heavenly Jerusalem and the earthly Babylon, and a supernatural grace and sin-stained nature pervade the Puritan imagination. The Puritan efforts to mediate these and other real or apparent polarities through their teaching on the convenant and their often-difficult attempts to develop a sacramental theology must be seen in light of their awareness of the urgent reality and power of an apocalyptic struggle between the divine and the demonic. Shepard's own imagination, imagery, and thought persistently try to locate the point or points of mediation through which such polarities may be comprehended if not entirely resolved. As one of the visibly called and gathered believers, Shepard presupposed that the way of faith is marked by dichotomies—in its vision of God's infinite power and transcendence and human contingency and finiteness, of an inexorable either/or logic in all questions spiritual, and of the encompassing kingdoms of God and Satan, grace and death, and gain and loss that ultimately define all earthly conflicts.

For Shepard as for the Puritans, God often assumes the designation of *Deus absconditus*—hidden, ineffable, and wholly transcendent in His mystery and power. As the Creator and ground of reality, the voice speaking to Job from the whirlwind, and the deliverer of the exiled remnant in the Old and New Testament, God is for Shepard a *mysterium tremendum* inspiring in his human creatures a response of awe and trembling.[19] What God's glorious essence is, writes Shepard, "no man or Angell hath, doth, or ever shall know; their cockle-shell can never comprehend this sea." But God's incomprehensible mystery "makes his glory to be the more admired, as wee admire the lustre of the Sunne the more, in that it is so great we cannot behold it."[20] In echoing the Augustinian and Calvinist emphasis on God's total sovereignty, Shepard envisions the human condition as limited, finite, contingent, and wholly dependent for its continued existence on God's grace and mercy. The persistent chasm between God's time (*kairos*) and human time (*kronos*) and between God's transcendent power and the earth-bound and sinful state of unregenerate man recurs as a dominant theme in Shepard's writings. Indeed, Shepard tries to find in his imagery a language that will allow him to speak in analogies about God and his relationship with creation—and allow him to discover God's image in nature and humanity—but at the same time he consistently preserves a vision of God that allows for his absolute freedom as the "wholly Other."

This pervasive Puritan sense of God's mysterious transcendence in contrast to the radical limitations of all things natural and human often borders on a stark dualism reminiscent of the Jansenist impulse and the series of contrasts and dichotomies between grace and nature, faith and reason, that find a later voice in Pascal. It is striking that even the Puritan form of logical discourse, which relies on the method of Peter Ramus, consistently utilizes a series of dichotomies rather than the tripartite form of the conventional Aristotelian syllogism. By embracing an either/or method of logical discourse, the Puritan mind intensified the habit of relying not so much on a "middle way" in questions of faith and reason but on a method utilizing sharply divergent contrasts at the heart of which lay the absolute contrast between truth and falsity. According to John Cotton, this "disjunctive" form of Ramist logic in which radical oppositions are prominent is sanctioned by God's own will: "the will of God towards the world is put forth in a disjunct axiome."[21] Election and reprobation, supernatural grace and unredeemed nature, light and darkness, and even the tension between God's justice and mercy as the Puritans envisioned it, are among the dialectical polarities that mark the Puritan mind and imagination. At the Last Judgment, says Shepard, God will not prove a Savior "if thou hast the superscription and Image of the devill, and not the Image of God upon thee. . . . Labour therefore to have *Gods* image restored againe, and Satans washt out" (40).

These sharply contrasting ideas and images reflect the intensity of the Puritan conviction that the center of history is spiritual and providential and that it reflects the constant struggle between the Kingdom of God and that of Satan. All kingdoms and cities are defined according to the object of their love, Augustine had argued in *The City of God* and elsewhere, and all human beings are citizens either of God's heavenly city of Jerusalem or of Satan's wordly Babylon. The first city is ruled by charity and faith, the second by self-love and prideful vanity. Luther and Calvin also insist on this distinction. In this world, writes Luther, we have no lasting citizenship and must "think of ourselves as travelers or pilgrims occupying for a night the same inn, eating and drinking there and leaving the place." Since all believers are "subjects of two kingdoms" and experience "two kinds of life," it is crucial to comprehend "the distinction between the kingdom of heaven and the kingdom of the world" and always to keep in mind "the kingdom whither we are bound."[22]

In their adherence to these distinctions and their specific emphases, and in their contention that Scripture dictates their truth, the Puritans remain in the mainstream of medieval and Reformation religious thought. The essence of Puritan doctrine is Reformed and Calvinist. In their rejection of Arminius and his followers and the "Arminian" movement which represented a break with the early, classical forms of Calvinist doctrine in favor of more "liberal" and less rigorous tenets, the Puritans considered Calvin one of their most vital and influential theologians and teachers. Puritan doctrine held to the Calvinist principles that God is totally free and sovereign; that man's will and intellect are wholly darkened and debilitated by the Fall; that Christ died for the elect and not to bring about universal salvation; that Scripture is the only rule and norm of faith and practice; that grace is irresistible and unconditional, given God's power and grace and man's unworthiness and lack of free will; and that God's predestined decrees will bring out of the wreckage and trials of this life the salvation of his persevering saints.

The Puritan understanding of and teaching on the sacraments of baptism and the Lord's Supper—the only two sacraments, or divinely instituted signs, Luther and Calvin acknowledged among the seven sacraments of the Roman Catholic church—are often complex. Edward Taylor's poetry celebrates the Eucharist as a manifestation of the Real Presence made efficacious by grace and faith, and so follows the emphasis Luther retained from the medieval church even while he rejected the church's doctrine of transubstantiation, or the indispensable efficacy of the priestly role in the Eucharist. Other Puritans deny the "physical force" of the Real Presence and adhere more closely to the Calvinist position that the Eucharist is a vital "sign and seal" of Christ's promise of salvation even though Christ's body is not literally present in the bread and wine. Still other Puritans echo Zwingli's conception of the Eucharist as a "memorial" to Christ rather than an efficacious and supernatural communion with him in the present. Despite these differences, however, the general Puritan doctrine of the sacraments as visible signs and seals of God's covenant with his people remains continuous with older forms of church tradition and teaching.

In light of these continuities of doctrine and piety between Puritanism and its Reformation and medieval roots, it is necessary to locate the radical difference between New England Puritanism and its religious antecedents in their respective understandings of the church. Although Augustine insists that the earthly and heavenly kingdoms must be distinguished from each other, he also notes that the citizens of each kingdom are "conmingled" in this world. Hence, he argues, even in the "city" that is the pilgrim church on earth, it is inevitable that the saved and the reprobate, the redeemed and the unrepentant, will be intermixed. The church is not composed solely of the regenerate, for God alone can look into each believer's heart and know all secret intentions. Rather, the church, like the world, holds in tension saints and sinners, wheat and chaff, until God's ultimate judgment separates them. The church is not a bastion of absolute purity, says Augustine, but a *corpus mixtum,* a mixed body. To insist otherwise, he concludes, is to elevate human judges into God's place and perspective and to risk separatism and schism by sects like the Donatists who proclaimed their own purity and salvation. The church, like the individual believer, must see itself as *justus et peccator,* saved and sinful, so long as it remains in its earthly form.

By admitting to church membership and to the sacraments those who made a profession of faith, were attentive to the Word of God and receptive to the sacraments, and sincere and persevering in their attempt to live a godly life, Augustine—and Luther and Calvin after him—assented to this conception of the earthly church. For them, as for the Puritans, the church was known by its rightful proclamation of the Word of God and by its rightful administration of the sacraments. But while Augustine and the early Reformers feared and denounced separatism and held that the earthly church as a city and kingdom could approximate, but not be wholly identical to, the City and Kingdom of God, the Puritan experiment in New England attempted to gather a covenanted church whose visible saints also were citizens of this supernatural and eternal Kingdom.

To be sure, the Puritans in old and New England also repudiated the various sects of Protestant Separatists. In New England, the Puritans consistently affirmed their allegiance to the Anglican communion. Nonetheless, their vision of their gathered church and setting as "a city upon a hill" appointed by God to illuminate and inspire the church in England and Europe presupposed a special providential calling. Separated from their brethren by an ocean, entering a new world through a literal and spiritual exodus, and placed in a wilderness at once physical and symbolic, it is no wonder that their professed solidarity with the Church of England would be tension-ridden and strained even had their respective doctrinal and political differences been less profound than they were at the time. The same Anglican order to which they expressed loyalty was to them in need of purifying and reform, for they believed that its rites and sacraments had become thoughtless and politicized forms of what Dietrich Bonhoeffer in our own time has called "cheap grace," or faith and discipleship without rigor, conviction, or cost. By gathering in the wilderness as a church of regenerate believers, the Puritans would constitute a witness to the reality of God's presence and claims. They would vindicate the conviction and hope, as Samuel Sewall described it even some forty years after Shepard's death, that the heart of America would be the foundation of the New Jerusalem.

Just as the Puritans recognized the dangers of separatism, so they acknowledged that ultimately the truly regenerate elect, the real members of the City of God, past, present, and future, were chosen by and known to God alone. Yet from the perspective of the New England Way, a profession of faith and an effort to lead a life of piety sufficed neither to admit candidates into church membership nor to participate in the Eucharist. In their determination to admit to membership only the truly regenerate—and to ask all potential members to give a persuasive account and testimony of their experience of saving grace—the Puritans went beyond the major tradition of the medieval and Reformation church as well as the Anglican communion and the great majority of the Puritans who remained in England. In his *Institutes,* Calvin like Augustine had argued that true regeneration comes about through the divine gift of grace in the form of a sense and conviction of the heart. This sense, he concluded, is "nothing other than what each believer experiences within himself."[23] New England's godly ministers would examine the testimony of potential church members for this experiential assurance and admit or disqualify such individuals according to the authenticity of their experience of faith and conversion. To the opponents of the New England experiment, such proceedings were at best presumptuous and questionable and at worst heretical; to Shepard, they were a vital part of God's design for his kingdom.

The spiritual and political intensity that scholars from Perry Miller to Sacvan Bercovitch have seen as characteristic of the Puritan experiment in New England plays an especially important role in this conception of the church. As the power of the polarities of experience impinged on the Puritan consciousness and imagination, the means of the Puritan way to faith and salvation—the Word; revelation; the grace of Christ's redemption; and the convenant—became not only critical but indispensable to the Puritan hope for assurance and peace. In *The Revolution of the Saints,* Michael Walzer states that the intensity of Puritanism comes in great measure from its essential denial of the intercessory vision of the Great Chain of Being and its hierarchies and gradations in favor of a more direct and experiential vision of man's need to respond directly and without intercession to God's will and commands. As Perry Miller had argued previously in a related way, the persistent focus of covenant theology from the Puritans through Edwards and even Emerson is "the Puritan's effort to confront, face to face, the image of a blinding divinity in the physical universe, and to look upon that universe without the intermediacy of ritual, of ceremony, of the Mass and the confessional."[24]

For Shepard and the Puritans, the starkness of this drama is fearful and moving. Poised between heaven and hell, sustained by God's promise and covenant but persistently besieged, the individual soul in its temporal state is always reminded of, and touched by, eternity. Further, its choices and condition have an apocalyptic significance. As Jonathan Edwards states, God's salvation of a single soul is a more wondrous work than his creation of the universe. Yet the drama of the soul extends to the drama of the church and the nation. Even as Shepard preached to a congregation of individuals, he preached to a gathered church and to the national soul. The great themes of sin, conversion, repentance, and salvation are for Shepard personal, ecclesiastical, and political. For him, God's voice—and Shepard's attempt to be its creaturely instrument—addresses at once the individual, the mystical body of his church, and those political bodies which inevitably remind us that the experiences of hope and affliction assume forms that are not only personal or divine but communal.

Chapter Three

Defending the New England Way: Shepard as Apologist

In addressing New England's social needs and conscience, Shepard utilized many literary forms: letters, polemics, Election sermons, and such series of extended sermons as *The Parable of the Ten Virgins*. Whatever the form, he consistently returns to his vision of God's special covenant with New England and the incessant need for his chosen people to participate in that covenant with repentance and gratitude. God's freely offered covenant of grace had sustained Abraham and his children, Israel's remnant, and the elect of Christ's new dispensation through the trials of the desert and wilderness. Now in New England, "a special people" unique in all the earth, as Peter Bulkeley described the Puritan remnant, needed to recall the source of their covenant and respond to Him by serving as a light to a world grown dark and corrupt. In *New England's Lamentation* and *A Defense of the Answer,* Shepard proclaimed and defended New England's special redemptive mission by pointing to the decline and corruption of the old religious order and claiming that the New England vision of a visible and illumined church constituted the only real hope for recovering the pure Christianity that had been subverted and cast aside.

These works, like *The Parable of the Ten Virgins,* demonstrate how closely linked are doctrine and life, sermon and experience, and religious vision and political order in the seventeenth century as a whole and Puritan New England in particular. As writings, they witness to Shepard's concern with the social, political, and eternal consequences of those forms of belief the Puritans named heretical and anathema. Primary among those beliefs is that set of convictions and tendencies called Antinomianism.

The theological issues marking the Antinomian controversy are varied and complex. Further, they have ancient roots in Western Christendom, and the tensions they reflect are also located in the turbulent doctrinal struggles of the early church and the recurring movements of radical religious sects throughout the Middle Ages and Reformation. But it is evident that Shepard, who like his colleagues was galvanized to oppose the opinions of Anne Hutchinson and to examine closely the apparent teachings of John Cotton that had influenced her thought, identified Antinomianism as a radically subjective and autonomous form of religious experience. The threat of Antinomianism cast into sharp relief the complex relationship between the dualities and even intense polarities that lie at the heart of Puritanism. In this crisis, the sense of duality was expressed in the relationship between justification and sanctification, or faith and good works, or, in the common Puritan form, the Covenant of Grace and the Covenant of Works. At the center of this relationship is the absolute polarity of salvation and reprobation and the experiential question of personal assurance: how do I know I am saved?

For Luther, salvation comes by faith and grace alone and not by works. Reminded that the Epistle of James insists that "faith, if it have no workes, is dead" (2:17, *GB*), Luther described James as an epistle of straw in order to emphasize the primacy of grace and faith. Essentially, the Puritans followed Luther's doctrinal emphasis and its similar importance in Calvin. Yet since the Puritans placed great stress on the significance of personal conversion and the individual's actual experience of grace, they also needed to address individual anxiety over the ultimate questions of personal assurance and election. As David D. Hall points out, Puritan preachers "could not resolve the problem by declaring that anxiety was inevitable":

> They had to provide some objective measure of grace, some outward sign of inner holiness. One such sign was sanctification, the daily course of living a godly life. Though the Puritans recognized that a hypocrite could simulate the life of righteousness, they reasoned that only the person whose heart had been transformed could sustain his obedience to the will of God. Outward behavior could therefore be taken as a sign—albeit a confusing one—of justification.[1]

From Shepard's perspective and that of the other ministers who prosecuted the Antinomians, any attempt to sever good works and living a godly life from the order of salvation and authentic conversion invited chaos. Works were not the ground of salvation. But they were part of salvation's dramatic process. If Antinomian doctrine were true, wrote Shepard, and the individual's conversion "must be without the sight of any grace, faith, holiness, or special change in himself, by immediate revelation in an absolute promise" (*A*, 65), then enthusiasm, self-delusion, and anarchy surely would reign. Special revelations would abound; actions would be drained of meaning; and the relationship between one's outward acts and inward state, however complex, would be destroyed. To separate faith wholly from works was to press duality beyond its legitimate boundaries.

In his sermons as in his considerations of prospective members for his congregation, Shepard ultimately seeks to avoid Antinomian subjectivism even though he prizes the actual experience of grace in each believer's heart.[2] While the experience of grace and salvation is individual, the authenticity of that experience must be weighed and evaluated by a corporate tradition, a common faith, and a transcendent and normative rule applied on earth and in fear and trembling by God's appointed minister. Direct as religious experience is, it demands a framework of order and even a certain form of hierarchical sanction in order to be fully realized. If the Puritans broke with Roman Catholicism and high Anglicanism, they rejected the Quakers as well and continued to see the assumptions and tendencies of all forms of Antinomian and Separatist movements as manifestations of Satan's legions.

New England's Lamentation

Like the lamentations of the Old Testament prophets over Israel's backsliding ways, Shepard's lament indicts and warns an ungodly people. In this instance, Shepard's apocalyptic warnings are directed toward "*Old Englands* present errours" and point to the desolation bound to follow if those errors are not set right. Shepard wrote *New England's Lamentation* in 1644 as a letter to a friend in England, and it was published in the following year. As the subtitle notes, the letter was prompted by the increase in England of several heresies, including Antinomianism and Separatism. In diagnosing this illness and providing remedies for the "infection" of these errors and heresies, Shepard consistently uses the metaphor of disease to emphasize the contrast between England's corruption and New England's spiritual health. By so doing, he elevates New England as a beacon and model for England's dangerously wayward tendencies.

In *Illness as Metaphor,* Susan Sontag points out that the pattern of associating disease with an evil and corrupt body politic has a long history.[3] In the sixteenth century, the word "pestilential" meant "morally baneful or pernicious," and the powerful allegorical imagination of the seventeenth century linked physical and spiritual ills—as well as their remedies—closely and persistently to each other. The image of Christ as a physician ministering to and healing sicknesses of body and spirit underlies these metaphors of disease and corruption, but often the promise of Christ's healing seems overshadowed by the raging distempers and divisions of the sickened national body, political or religious, to which the prophet points. Shepard's vision of England's endangered state is intense and sustained: "Such cracks and flawes in the new building of Reformation, portend a fall; such hot fevers and inflammations of *Englands* languishing body, call to the Physitians to let out more blood before it can recover."[4]

These "deep distempers" (2), Shepard continues, are symptoms of a deeper disease of ungodliness whose only cure and remedy will be God's apocalyptic intervention and the emergence of a remnant of believers: "The Lord Christ will not passe by without darkning the Sunne, and turning the Moone into blood, which will and shall continue, untill the Lord hath made the remnant which shall escape, a poor, weak, humble, pliable spirited people, unto the good wayes of his grace" (2). In the course of *New England's Lamentation,* Shepard makes clear that this remnant is already present in New England and that it has forged a visible church to whose light and example England's beleaguered faithful may look with hope. The same scourges now afflicting England have been overcome in New England, argues Shepard, and any reports that the visible church and the holy experiment are themselves divided are "fables": "The Churches are here in peace; The Common wealth in peace; The ministry in most sweet peace. . . . All our families in peace." Yet, he concludes, "this peace giveth us no rest, while our deare *England* is in trouble, for which we would weep, and we with our heads fountaines in this wildernesse, for our sins there as well as others" (6). Even as Shepard distinguishes New England from its homeland, the intensity of the bonds and dialectic between them remains clear. The "infections" of Antinomianism, schism, and disorder may have diminished in New England as they simultaneously and severely afflict the English political and church body, but as scourges they clearly constitute a "common Enemy" (2).

A Defense of the Answer

In imploring God's merciful intercession and England's repentance in *New England's Lamentation,* Shepard affirms the example of the New England Way as the model form of church government. Yet during the 1630s many English Puritans had gravitated to a Presbyterian ecclesiastical structure, with a centralized authority, and came to view with suspicion and skepticism the Puritan experiment in New England. Already critical of the zeal with which the ministerial leaders of that experiment examined prospective candidates for church membership and uncertain about the precise nature of the visible church as it would be defined in New England, they also questioned the Congregational model Shepard and his fellow ministers championed. By providing far greater autonomy to each congregation than did the Presbyterian form of government, they feared, a real Presbyterian reformation and a coherent and stable church order would prove impossible. In 1636, John Ball, an English divine who supported Presbyterianism, addressed to the New England ministry on behalf of the Presbyterian cause a series of nine questions or positions. Ball demanded that Shepard and others clarify the nature of the "Catholick visible Church" they sought to establish by answering a series of doctrinal questions on church structure and procedure.

John Davenport in 1639 responded to Ball's questions and accusations in *An Answer of the Elders of the Several Churches in New England unto Nine Positions Sent over to Them.* This rejoinder, published in 1643, set out in detail a Congregational structure of church government; defended the New England order; and attempted to answer in a systematic way the accusations Ball had brought against the procedures of that order. Ball, now certain that the Puritans had in fact betrayed—or had never intended to adopt—the Presbyterian ecclesiastical form, attacked Davenport's *Answer.* In turn, Shepard and John Allin prepared *A Defense of the Answer* in order to counter Ball's polemic and to justify once more the Puritan mission in New England. The work, which appeared in 1648, stands as an immensely important affirmation of the Puritan spirit in its new setting.

Ball's *Nine Questions* and Davenport's *Answer* centered on such critical issues as the order of worship, liturgical rituals, the sacraments, the ministerial role, standards for church membership, the act of excommunication, and other ecclesiastical and doctrinal matters. Although *A Defense of the Answer* clearly springs from and is an integral part of these same concerns, it also reaches beyond particular doctrinal disputes and complexities through the impassioned language and vision of Shepard's preface. In his preface, Shepard delineates New England Puritanism as part of a cosmic drama. Further, he insists that its foundation and direction within that drama is not innovative but restorative. By recovering and restoring the essence of faith, form, and practice as it had existed in the dawn of Christianity, Shepard states, the Puritan errand could provide the culmination of the Reformation and serve as God's vehicle for redeeming the time. As Cotton Mather would write a half-century later, "The *First Age* was the *Golden Age:* To return unto *That,* will make a man a *Protestant,* and I may add, a *Puritan.*"[5]

Shepard and the other Puritan ministers were to argue that the rigor of their examination of prospective church members was consistently tempered by mercy and charity. But in his preface Shepard strongly affirms the importance of instituting just such an examination. He acknowledges that "in receiving to our Churches onely visible Saints and beleevers," the New England Way that would be articulated in the Cambridge Platform seemed to break with the practices of the Reformation churches. But their determination to build and sustain this kind of visible church, writes Shepard, is steadfast: "We thinke reformation of the Church doth not onely consist in purging out corrupt Worship, and setting up the true; but also in purging the Churches from such profanenesse and sinfulnesse as is scandalous to the Gospel, and makes the Lord weary of his owne Ordinances."[6] In the rhetoric of polarity so central to the Puritan spirit, Shepard emphasized that light and darkness, Christ and Satan, and the truly converted and the unregenerate simply cannot coexist in Christ's own church. The orthodoxy of New England will constitute a return to the purity of early Christianity, counter the heresies and lukewarmness of the present age, and witness to the entire world: "Sent into this Wildernesse to beare witnesse to [Christ's] truth, it is unto us reward sufficient, that we should be witnesses thereunto, even to the utmost parts of the Earth" (1).

In stressing the global nature of New England's mission into the wilderness, Shepard takes great pains to recall that God, not man, is the true and sole author of the enterprise. By offering his gracious covenant to the Puritans, and by sustaining the weak but persevering faithful through the trials of sea and wilderness, God has nurtured a miraculous event: "Look from one end of the heaven to another, whether the Lord hath assayed to do such a Worke as this in any Nation, so to carry out a people of his owne from so flourishing a State, to a wildernesse so far distant, for such ends, and for such a worke" (6). In biblical prose and imagery, Shepard celebrates God's sustaining power and mercy:

> What shall we say of the singular Providence of God bringing so many Ship-loads of his people, through so many dangers, as upon Eagles wings, with so much safety from yeare to yeare? [Of] The fatherly care of our God in feeding and cloathing so many in a Wildernesse . . . what shall wee say of the Worke it selfe of the kingdome of Christ? and the form of a Common-wealth erected in a Wildernesse, and in so few yeares brought to that state, that scarce the like can bee seen in any of our English Colonies in the richest places of this *America,* after many more years standing? (7–8)

By appealing as consistently as he does to God's providential covenant with New England, Shepard clearly indicates that he envisions history as *Heilsgeschichte,* or a pattern of events rooted in divine guidance and intercession. No less than in Edward Johnson's later *Wonder-Working Providence of Sions Saviour in New England* (1654) and Cotton Mather's *Magnalia Christi Americana* (1702), Shepard's vision of God's redeeming and providential history is centered in an apocalyptic drama: "Wee cannot see but the rule of Christ to his Apostles and Saints, and the practice of Gods Saints in all ages, may allow us this liberty . . . to fly into the Wildernesse from the face of the Dragon" (4). For Shepard, this Dragon must be associated not only with the old Anglican order or those Presbyterians accusing the New England Puritans of the sin of Separatism, but with all the forces of anarchy, dissolution, idolatry, and satanic corruption that coalesce into a vision of the Antichrist.

To be sure, Shepard makes it clear that England's religious situation is the ground and catalyst for these wider and deeper disorders. The kingdom of Christ, he contends, is hardly likely to emerge in England, for "there is no more regard of the solemn

Covenant, especially in personall reformation, then if it were never made. . . . Oh *England! England!* our beloved *England!* wilt thou not be made cleane?" (23). In marked contrast to the diminished or even absent covenant in England stands New England's "nationall Covenant" (18) with God and among each other. For Shepard, only "Gods Providence first and last" has allowed New England's Puritanism to engage in "the great worke of this age" and in the "nick of time" (2–3). Without this reformation and restoration of the true church, all would have been lost:

> For was it not a time when humane Worship and inventions were growne to such an intolerable height, that the consciences of Gods saints and servants inlightened in the truth . . . could no longer bear them? Was not the power of the tyrannicall Prelates so great, that like a strong Current carryed all down streame before it, what ever was from the law, or otherwise set in their way? Did not the hearts of men generally fail them? (3)

The intensity of Shepard's questions stems in part from his need to respond to the charge that the Puritans who emigrated to New England were "rash" or "hasty" in their decision. On the contrary, insists Shepard, they were prudent, purposeful, and fully aware of the cost in pain and suffering: "And what if God will have his Church and the Kingdome of Christ goe up also in these remote parts of the world . . . surely all were not rash, weake-spirited, inconsiderate of what they left behinde, or of what it was to goe into a Wildernesse" (6). Their journey was a trial, for it meant leaving many friends and relatives, facing the "dangers and difficulties of the vast Seas, the thought whereof was a terrour to many" (7), and entering "a wildernesse, where we could forecast nothing but care and temptations, onely in hopes of enjoying Christ in his Ordinances, in the fellowship of his people" (7). No one could undertake such a mission and trial from careless motives: "No surely, with what bowells of compassion to our deare Countrey; with what heart-breaking affection, to our deare relations . . . the Lord is witnesse" (7). Even as Shepard's voice is prophetic and apocalyptic, it remains deeply human.

The human resonance of Shepard's voice is engendered by the profundity of his own experience and that of the Puritan movement to and in New England. Although the habit of seeing and interpreting all experience in a typological and allegorical way finds its source in Scripture and in its interpretation by St. Augustine and others, there can be no doubt that this method of seeing was given new force and power by the Puritans' literal, tangible experience of the ancient biblical images. Shepard points to a real voyage of exodus through an actual sea into a literal wilderness. As allegorical and apocalyptic as his images are, they are rooted in that literal reality from which all authentic allegory proceeds. The "literal sense" of Shepard's diction, imagery, and imagination, like the literal sense of Scripture, remains the foundation for his vision and claim.

A significant part of the power of Shepard's vision and the intensity of his voice in the preface to *A Defense of the Answer* resides in a certain tenor of suffering. If the preface is a proclamation of the Puritan mission, Shepard proclaims it while fully aware of its cost and sacrifice. In his description of their trials and separations, Shepard counters any temptation to envision the emigrating Puritans as easily triumphant. On the contrary, here as elsewhere they persevere only because of their faith and God's intercession, and both their faith and their ability to see and interpret divine guidance continue to be tested and tried. Even Shepard's conception of Christ is based on this sense of pain and suffering. As a commentator has remarked in a more contemporary setting, the mystery of the Incarnation is the common ground from which two vectors in the Christian tradition originate and then diverge. One centers on the glory of the Christ of the Nativity and Resurrection as it illuminates and transfigures an otherwise fallen world. The second emphasizes "in the Incarnation and humiliation of the physical being, a model of suffering assumed" and moves toward Christ "by the Way of the Cross."[7] The Puritan tradition and Shepard himself are capable of celebrating the sacramental aspect of the Christian faith and of joyously proclaiming both Nativity and Resurrection. Yet their sense of the Crucifixion and of the cost and pain of discipleship—in history, in external events, and within themselves—constitutes their starting point. If the New England Way will ultimately triumph, Shepard contends, it will do so only through the suffering way of the Cross, and only through the intercession of God's sustaining covenant.

Chapter Four

Law, Gospel, and Covenant: The Puritan Faith

When Greenhill and Mather remarked in their assessment of Shepard's works that "Law-Sermons" were indispensable to "Gospel-lives," they presupposed the importance of the link between Law and Gospel in the Christian tradition. Luther insists that one cannot be a theologian without being able to distinguish between Law—including the Mosaic law of the Old Testament and the natural law apart from Christ—and the Gospel of Christ's grace and salvation. The first, writes Luther, often stands in absolute contrast to the second even though Christ came to "fulfill" rather than to "abolish" the Law. Indeed, John Bunyan consistently associates the old law and covenant with wrath and death and the new law with the life and grace of Christ: "The word of the law and wrath must give place to the word of life and grace; because, though the word of condemnation be glorious, yet the word of life and salvation doth far exceed in glory . . . Moses and Elias must both vanish, and leave Christ and his saints alone."[1] Yet just as the Old Testament prefigured the New Testament and Moses prefigured Christ's coming and illimined Christ's significance, so for the Puritans "the bright glass of the Law wherein we may see the evil of sin" remains a crucial necessity in the work of preaching and conversion: "How shall wee come to the right sight of our sinnes, and a sound perswasion of the greatness of them? By the spirit of God leading us into the true understanding of the law, and a due examination of ourselves thereby."[2]

By insisting that "if we cleave to the law, we are bereft of all blessing and a curse hangs over us," Calvin unequivocally affirms man's inability to keep the law through his own virtue and good works: "The Lord promises nothing except to perfect keepers of his law, and no one of the kind is to be found": "The fact, then, remains that through the law the whole human race is proved subject to God's curse and wrath, and in order to be freed from these, it is necessary to depart from the power of the law and . . . to be released from its bondage into freedom."[3] An awareness and apprehension of the Law must precede any saving knowledge and experience of the Gospel. Further, as Calvin states, the promises of Law and Gospel are in essential agreement.[4] By emphasizing the importance of the Law, the Puritans at once make it part of the process of conversion and repudiate those who, like the Antinomians, believe that the experience of faith and grace alone (justification) makes irrelevant the subsequent habit and practice of good works (sanctification). Even after the saving act of faith, as Ernest F. Kevan remarks, "the continuation of the believer's moral obligation to fulfill the law is one of the most established of the Puritan convictions."[5] Yet the polarities inherent in the Puritan mind and imagination are always close to the surface of this doctrinal question. In *The Sincere Convert* and *The Sound Believer,* Shepard discusses and dramatizes the need for God's covenant and man's conversion against the backdrop of polarities: election and reprobation, light and darkness, freedom and imprisonment, and the natural, unregenerate soul and the soul transformed and regenerate.

The Sincere Convert

Of these two works, *The Sincere Convert* is the earlier (1641) and the more stark and controversial. Its subtitle—"Discovering the Paucity of True Beleevers; And the great difficulty of *Saving Conversion*"—sets the work's tone. An English divine and sometime critic of Shepard, Giles Firmin, describes "the general part" of *The Sincere Convert* as "very solid, quick, and searching." It "cuts very sharply," he continues, and "is not a book for an unsound heart to delight in, I mean, in those places where he agrees both with Scriptures, and with other able Divines, and of these makes use." But other passages dealing with the infinitesimal number of elect and the agonizing difficulty of preparing the heart for real conversion, Firmin indicates, are in harmony neither with Scripture nor compassion. One of Firmin's acquaintances even tells him that "he had a Maid-servant who was very godly, and reading . . . in Mr. *Shepherd's* Book, which I opposed, she was so cast down, and fell into such troubles that all the Christians that came to her could not quiet her spirit."[6]

When he wrote to Shepard to question certain of his doctrines, states Firmin, Shepard informed him that he did not even possess a copy of *The Sincere Convert*: "Mr. *Shepherd's* own words in his Letter to me . . . are these . . . *That which is called the* Sincere Convert, *I have not the book, I once saw it; it was a Collection of such Notes in a dark Town in* England, *which one procuring of me, published them without my will . . . I scarce know what it contains.*"[7] In noting that Shepard wrote the letter in 1647, Firmin also ridicules the possibility that the 1646 edition of *The Sincere Convert* had in fact been "corrected and much amended" by "the Author" as the title page claimed. Indeed, the several editions of *The Sincere Convert* published shortly after the original text in 1641 are actually reprintings rather than new editions and clearly had not been revised by Shepard.

Yet it is significant that in corresponding with Firmin, Shepard did not disclaim responsibility for all of the points of doctrine on which Firmin challenged him but apparently defended certain of them vigorously. Further, the practice by which parishoners took sermon notes and then arranged for their publication—sometimes without even informing their preacher—was quite common. For Firmin, the doctrinal difficulties in *The Sincere Convert* remain vexing despite Shepard's general response. Firmin simply concludes his comments on *The Sincere Convert* by taking note of Shepard's extraordinary intensity and by distinguishing between *The Sincere Convert* and *The Sound Believer*. His father-in-law once told him, says Firmin, that when Shepard "*comes to deal with Hypocrites, he cuts so desperately that we know not how to bear him, made them all afraid, that they were all Hypocrites: when he came to deal with a tender humble Soul, he gives comfort so largely, that we are afraid to take it. I* let that reverend Author then alone, he is one on our side, in his *Sound Believer,* which he himself put forth."[8]

Although the claim that many of his listeners were even afraid to accept Shepard's solace because of its apparently dreadful power was clearly not widespread, the intensity of Shepard's prose in *The Sincere Convert* is striking. Shepard's tone and imagery are relentlessly animated and "affective," as when he describes God's omnipresence through the images of theatre and book: "It's no matter what thy fellow Actors on this stage of the world imagine. God is the great Spectator that beholds thee in every place; God is thy spye, and takes compleate notice of all the actions of thy life; and they are in print in heaven, which that great spectator and Judge will open at the great day, and reade alowd in the eares of all the World" (20). In light of the real presence of God's all-seeing omniscience, says Shepard, it is clear that salvation is a "hard matter" and that "God hath not lined the way to Christ with velvet" (145):

> The gate is straight, and therefore a man must sweat and strive to enter; both the entrance is difficult, and the progresse of salvation too. Jesus Christ is not got with a wet finger. It is not wishing and desiring to be saved, will bring men to heaven; hells mouth is full of good wishes. It is not shedding a teare at a Sermon, or blubbering now and then in a corner, and saying over thy prayers, and crying God[s] mercy for thy sinnes, will save thee. (144)

Shepard's powerful tone and images—the "wet finger" refers to a purely abstract notion of salvation such as might be gained by a reader idly turning a book's pages with a moistened finger—persistently invoke an absolute distinction between the unregenerate and regenerate soul and between the true believer and the hypocrite. These polarities underlie and pervade *The Sincere Convert.* Shepard embraces the Calvinist emphasis on man's utter depravity of intellect and will, or his inability through his own powers to know the truth and do the good, and always implicit in Shepard's language is the Pauline lament: "For I knowe, that in me . . . dwelleth no good thing: for to wil is present in me: but I finde no meanes to performe that which is good. For I do not the good thing, which I wolde, but the evil, which I wolde not, that do I" (Rom. 7:18–19; *GB*).

From this emphasis come many of Shepard's most powerful and evocative images. While there remains in William Perkins and William Ames and other Puritan theologians a mistrust of visual images in the order of worship—a Reformed confession of the sixteenth century approvingly quotes Lactantius's assertion that "undoubtedly no religion exists where there is an image"—the imagistic and imaginative dimensions of Puritan sermons are often strong, and in Shepard's works they are effective and pervasive. The eye is the devil's door, says John Donne, while the ear is the Holy Ghost's first door, and for the Puritan imagination, steeped in the Pauline doctrine that faith comes by hearing, Donne's distinction is seminal. Yet that same Puritan imagination consistently utilizes visual imagery in rhetorical frameworks and settings and especially in its sermons, as in Shepard's description of the imprisonment of the natural or unregenerate soul: "Every naturall man is damned in Heaven and damned on earth":

God is thy all-seeing terrible Judge: Conscience is thine accuser; an heavie witnesse: His word is thy Jayle: thy lusts are thy Fetters: In this Bible is pronounced and writ thy doome, thy sentence: Death is thy hangman, and that fire that shall never goe out, thy torment: The Lord hath in his infinite patience reprived thee for a time; O take heed and get a pardon before the day of execution come[s]. (66)

It is telling that the encompassing setting for these legal and judicial images is the Law and its attendant terrors for those "co[n]demned in the court of Gods justice, by the law which cryes *treason, treason,* against the most high God, & condemned by justice & mercy by the Gospel, which cryes murder murder against the sonne of God" (65–66).

In his description of the fallen soul "fettered by the difficulties of his desires" and "because of his shackles unable to walk on the way," St. Augustine located a similar experience of pain and imprisonment: "He feels himself in fetters; he cries unto the Lord."[9] Yet the apocalyptic severity of man's corruption and the Law's shadow and judgment in *The Sincere Convert* is still more relentless. For some hard-hearted unbelievers, says Shepard, even the moment of death cannot engender true repentance:

Nay commonly then mens hearts are most hard, and therefore men dye like Lambes, and cry not out; Then it's hard plucking thy soule from the Devils hands, to whom thou hast given it all thy life by sinne, and if thou dost get it back, dost thou thinke that God will take the devils leavings? Now thy day is past, and darknesse begins to over-spread thy soule; now flocks of Devils come into thy chamber, waiting for thy soul, to flye upon it as a Mastive Dog when the doore is opened. (72)

For Shepard, the state of sin underlying and informing this spirit of disbelief and resistance to God is organic and pervasive: "Every naturall man and woman is borne full of all sin . . . as full as a Toade is full of poison, as full as ever his skin can hold; Minde, Will, Eyes, Mouth, every limbe of his body, and every piece of his soul is full of sin" (51).

As powerful as Shepard's tone and imagery are, of course, and quite apart from the question of how much of *The Sincere Convert* he would have sanctioned had he been able to prepare it for publication, Shepard's dramatization of the terror of God's wrath and the precarious state of the unregenerate soul living under the Law's accusatory judgment are expressions of traditional Puritan doctrine. Even Giles Firmin acknowledges the solidity of "the general part" of *The Sincere Convert.* In his intense descriptions of the soul's desperation before the Law, Shepard was giving tangible form to the early stages of the "morphology" of conversion as William Perkins had set it out.[10] The experience of faith and grace through conversion constitutes for the Puritan mind the only source for the soul's "pardon" and "reprieve." By attending to the Word and coming to a knowledge of the Law, the aspiring believer might then become aware of his own specific sins and reach a "legall feare," or state of self-conviction and humiliation. After moving through these preparatory steps, the elect would then experience further degrees of conviction and real conversion: a serious attending on the Gospel's promise; the will and faith to believe; a struggle against doubt and despair; a sense of assurance through Christ's mercy; a sorrow for sin born from true grief and piety; and a reception of that grace that would provide the means of sanctification by which he would be obedient to God's will and commands. Even in these last stages of assurance, Perkins insists, the conflict between faith and doubt in the believing soul continues, though grace and salvation will ultimately triumph.

In *The Sincere Convert,* Shepard clearly holds out the promise and possibility of ultimate salvation even as he delineates the terror of the Law: "As the Glasse set full against the sunne receives not onely the beames, as all other darke bodies doe, but the image of the sunne: So the understanding with open face beholding Christ, is turned into the Image and likenesse of *Christ*": "Men now adayes looke only to the best mens lives, and see how they walk, and rest here; o looke higher to this blessed face of God in Christ, as thine owne; As the application of the seale to the waxe imprints the Image, so to view the grace of Christ, as *all* thine, imprints the same image strongly on the soule" (41). Shepard's exhortations and imagery reflect not only a sense of the real possibility of conversion but an embracing of a sacramental vision of the relationship between Christ and humanity in which Christ's image is bestowed on an earthly creature. This emphasis is that of the Puritan poet Edward Taylor, and it resonates with the hope and assurance that the hidden God would not only reveal Himself through Christ to the believer but that He would do so in love. With this presupposition, and in this setting, the Law's terrors are an indispensable part of the heart's preparation for faith, grace, and conversion in the same way that darkness prepares the way for light and death the way for resurrection.[11]

Yet it is not difficult to understand Firmin's questions about aspects of the arguments and expositions in *The Sincere Convert.* Shepard implies that there are times when the very act of repentance may be made impossible by the depth of the heart's corruption. The elect are few in number and conversion is an immensely difficult process. The "blessed face of God in Christ" may be "thine owne," but seemingly more emphatic and persistent in *The Sincere Convert* is the presence of the omnipotent God whose face is hidden from the despairing soul: "Oh I might once have had mercy and Christ, but no hope now ever to have one glimpse of his face, or one good looke from him any more" (94). Adam's sin with its communal guilt, the power of Satan, and God's sovereign justice and righteousness as they confront the unregenerate soul are Shepard's persistent concerns. God clearly is merciful as well as just: "God is not all Mercy and no Justice, nor all Justice and no Mercy. Submit to him, his mercy embraceth thee. Resist him, his justice pursues thee" (23–24). But neither believer nor unbeliever should treat this mercy casually, insists Shepard, for fear and trembling are requisite conditions for any authentic response to God: "O feare this God when you come before him. People come before God in Prayer, as before their fellowes, or as before an Idoll. People tremble not at his voyce in the Word. A King or Monarch will bee served in state, yet how rudely, how slovenly do men goe about every holy duty" (24).

Whether invoking the stern tone of the jeremiad or a more solicitous tone of consolation, Shepard's intensity in *The Sincere Convert* is sustained throughout. Underlying this intensity and in part generating it is the Puritan emphasis—and one to which Shepard especially subscribes—on God as Redeemer rather than on God as Creator. This emphasis reverberates with significance for Shepard's conception of time and for his dramatization of the existential depths of the soul in its encounter with Christ.

Like St. Thomas Aquinas, who places great importance on God's essential name of Creator, and like Calvin, who begins his *Institutes* by insisting that God's revelation in the work of creation makes inexcusable any denial of Him as the Creator of the universe, Shepard begins his reflections on God in *The Sincere Convert* by affirming that God is "glorious in his *Works* . . . of Creation, and in his workes of providence and government" (24). In images that Edward Taylor later echoed in the preface to *Gods Determinations Touching His Elect* and that find their original source in Genesis, Job, and the Psalms, Shepard vividly praises God as the architect and creator who sustains his creation: If we see a stately house, says Shepard, we know "some wise Artificer hath beene working here":

> can wee when we behold the stately theater of Heaven and Earth, conclude other, but that the finger, armes, and wisdome of God hath beene here, although we see not him that is invisible, and although we know not the time when he began to build. Every creature in heaven and earth is a loud preacher of this Truth: who set those candles, those torches of heaven on the Table? who hung out those lanthornes in heaven to enlighten a darke world? . . . could any frame a man, but one wiser and greater than man? . . . who sends the Sun post from one end of heaven to the other, carrying so many thousand blessings to so many thousands of people and King-domes? what power of man or Angels can make the least pile of grasse, or put life into the least fly, if once dead? (4)

Shepard's acknowledgment and celebration of God's wisdom and power in creating and sustaining the order of the universe are impressive.

Yet as Georges Poulet has pointed out, the seventeenth century is the epoch in which the individual recognizes with a new sense of urgency and dread his isolation and contingency. The sense of duration that had been part of the vision of God as creator now collapses, for "God seemed less to prolong human existence continually than to hold over man from moment to moment an act of vengeance and annihilation."[12] Anxious over the discontinuities of experience and tortured by an awareness of the chasm into which he might fall at any instant, the individual feels as if he is suspended over an abyss without God's sustaining hand. "The creation," states Poulet, "no longer appeared the cardinal event in the history of the world. For the first time it was no longer the ground upon which human existence was established. Human existence rested no longer in God-the-creator-and-preserver but in God-the-redeemer."[13]

Despite Shepard's affirmation of God's creating and sustaining power, his most significant emphasis is precisely on God's act of redemption in Christ. In this act, the unregenerate soul is without certainty and duration unless and until Christ intercedes. Many of Shepard's most intense and terrifying images in *The Sincere Convert* describe this sense of helpless contingency, as in a passage that Jonathan Edwards echoed in *Sinners in the Hands of an Angry God.* God is a consuming fire against the unregenerate, says Shepard, and "there is but one paper wall of thy body between thy soule and eternall flames": "How soone may God stop thy breath, there is nothing but that betweene thee and hell; if that were gone, then farewell all. Thou art condemned, and the muffler is before thine eyes, God knowes how soone the ladder may be turned, thou hangest by one rotten twined thread of thy life over the flames of hell every houre" (70–71). Conscious of their radical contingency and of the precarious thread of life by which they hang over damnation, the unregenerate understandably despair of hope and salvation.

Only the process of regeneration could recover for the elect both a sense of duration and salvation. In the predestining will of God, writes Poulet, lies the only complete stability and consistency. By an act of absolute faith, the regenerate soul experiences the cojoining of this particular moment with an eternal moment and duration. Given his faith in the validity of the divine promise, "the whole existence of the just becomes thereafter the continuing act by which a divine unalterable will is superimposed upon a human duration incessantly failing. It is the permanence of eternity, constantly impressing itself upon the discontinuity of human moments."[14]

For Shepard, only faith in the blood of Christ's redemption can invoke this duration and coherence, for the soul cannot "make thy selfe a Christ for thy selfe" (104). In one of the most powerful and evocative passages in *The Sincere Convert,* he repudiates the idea that salvation might be generated apart from an absolute and unconditional faith in Christ's sacrifice. If you have not Christ, he insists, desire and pray "till thou hast worne thy tongue to the stumps" and "*mourne* in some Wildernesse till doomes day, digge thy grave there with thy nayles, weepe buckets full of hourely teares, till thou canst weepe no more":

> *Fast* and *pray* till thy skin and bones cleave together; *Promise* and *Purpose,* with full resolution to be better; nay *reforme* thy head, heart, life, & tongue, & some, nay all sinnes; live like an Angell, shine like a sunne, walke up and downe the world like a distressed Pilgrim going to another Countrey, so that all Christians commend and admire thee. Die ten thousand deaths,

lie at the firebacke in Hell so many millions of yeares as there be piles of grasse on the earth, or sands upon the Sea-shore, or starres in heaven, or motes in the Sun: I tell thee, not one sparke of Gods wrath against thy sinne shall be, can be quenched by all these *duties,* nor by any of these sorrowes, or *teares;* for, these are not the blood of Christ. Nay if all the Angels and Saints in heaven and earth should pray for thee, these cannot deliver thee, for they are not the blood of Christ. (104–5)

Only a personal response in faith to Christ's offer of salvation, and not a catalog of good works, no matter how impressive or sustained, can ensure Christ's "great worke of saving thee" (106).

The stark power of *The Sincere Convert* is directed throughout to the listener's and reader's affections even as it discusses matters of doctrine. In his attempt "to leade you so farre, as to shew you the rockes and dangers of your passage to another world" (266), Shepard clearly has in mind the Pauline voyage to "faith and a good conscience, which some have put away, and as concerning faith, have made shipwracke" (1 Tim. 1:19; *GB*). In *The Sincere Convert,* the soul's journey from a lost to a regenerate state through conflicting polarities is not only fearsome but terrifying. If the end of that journey—faith in and through the assurance of Christ's mercy and salvation—is not always as clear and compelling as the journey's Satanic terrors and imminent and tactile sense of damnation, it may well be owing to the circumstances by which *The Sincere Convert* was published. In any event, it is clear that in *The Sound Believer,* which, as Firmin noted, Shepard "himself put forth" and which is more centrally traditional in its emphasis on Gospel as well as Law and on grace as well as sin, Shepard's tone and expositions of doctrine are more modulated and sustained. In it, Shepard attributes to one major conception in Puritan doctrine a vital place it does not have in *The Sincere Convert:* the covenant of grace in its seminal, intercessory, and redemptive power.

The Sound Believer

In preparing *The Sound Believer* for its eventual publication in 1645, Shepard clearly had reservations. He himself thinks "more meanly of it than others can" and will not be sorry if the work is buried in "perpetuall silence" rather than seeing its way into print. But since he does wish to serve as Christ's voice and since the work will reach many friends and strangers he would not otherwise meet in this world, he indicates, he has "at last been perswaded." He gives full consent to the editing of his text so long as the process is "not crosse to what I have writ"—here recalling, perhaps, the controversy over *The Sincere Convert.* As a "Treatise of Evangelicall Conversion," *The Sound Believer* seeks to discover and delineate "The Work of Christs Spirit, in reconciling of a Sinner to God." This subtitle then takes for its epigraph Christ's words in Matthew 18:11: *"I came to save that which was lost."*

The essential structure of *The Sound Believer* is based on an analysis of the process of regeneration from the soul's state of loss and despair to that time when it is "wrapt up in Gods Covenant" (169). Shepard's delineation of this process takes as its starting point Perkins's descriptions of the soul's movement from its conviction of sin to its humiliation for sin and the beginnings of the act of faith. But unlike *The Sincere Convert, The Sound Believer* emphasizes as fully as the state of despair and anxiety the "blessed and happy estate" of redemption by which the elect are pardoned for their sins (justification); brought to peace with God (reconciliation); made sons of God (adoption); restored to God's image (sanctification); and the glorification in which they are ushered into the kingdom of heaven "in eternall Communion with God."[15] The starkness of the relationship between Christ and the soul in *The Sincere Convert* here gives way to an exploration of the mediating covenant of grace that provides an eternal duration amid the anxieties of the moment and an assurance of election and salvation amid terror and despair. For those souls "wrapt up" in the covenant, freedom overcomes imprisonment and Christ's grace the power of Satan.

The Puritan conceptions of the covenant of grace, like their conceptions of the church and civil covenants or their distinction between the covenant of works engendered by the fallen Adam and the covenant of faith engendered by Christ, are complex.[16] Questions over the internal and external covenants and over whether God's covenant of grace is absolute and unconditional—that is, an eternal and mediating grace wholly unrelated to the faithfulness or apostasy of its recipients—or conditional on the responsiveness of those seeking to live by it, persisted. Further, such questions affected individual Puritan divines as they formulated their sacramental theology on Baptism and the Lord's Supper. For Shepard, however, it is clear that God's covenant of grace with his elect is ultimately unconditional and that as a mediating instrument of his grace from Abraham to the present moment it illuminates, vivifies, and sustains his saints. The covenant is rooted in God's free promise of salvation through Christ's suffering and Resurrection, continually recalled and sealed through "the voice of the Gospel" (182) and the sacraments, and made permanent by the efficacious power of Christ's redemptive love. The animating principle of *The Sound Believer* is Samuel Willard's exhortation that "while a Saviour calls, and warns, and invites you, make haste, give no rest to your eyes, nor give him any rest, until you are gotten under the shadow of his wings, and set free from the condemnation of hell."[17] Its ideal end and resolution is also Willard's: "If any in the World have reason to rejoyce, you are they. It is a shame, to see an Heir of Damnation jocund, and a Child of God disconsolate. . . . Joy will be your Everlasting Employment hereafter, begin it then now, and so anticipate the Felicities of the Eternal Kingdom."[18]

Yet even in light of the dominant tone and direction of *The Sound Believer,* Shepard insists that the soul's awareness of sin must precede and be bound to any subsequent sense of mercy and joy: "Gospel Grace cannot be set out, much lesse felt, but in reference to sin and misery, which must be first felt, before it can be sweet" (62). This emphasis on the experiential dimension of sin and faith once again takes the form of Shepard's persistent distinction between an abstract and real understanding of faith's essence. As in *Ineffectual Hearing,* Shepard stresses this contrast:

> There is a reall light in spirituall conviction, rationall conviction makes things appear notionally; but spirituall conviction, really: the Spirit indeed useth argumentation in conviction, but it goes farther and causeth the soule not only to see sin and death discursively, but also intuitively and really: reason can see and discourse about words and Propositions, and behold things by report, and so deduct one thing from another; but the Spirit makes a man see the things themselves really wrapt up in those words; the Spirit brings spirituall things as well as notions before a mans eye, the light of the Spirit is like the light of the Sun, it makes all things appeare as they are. (26)

Neither sin nor faith nor salvation is for Shepard an abstraction. All are real, and spiritual conviction enables the word to be connected to the thing in such a way that language and reality "appeare as they are."

In describing the process of conversion in light of the Gospel, then, Shepard also invokes the Law. He must preach "the remedy" for sin, but "first preach the woe and misery of men, or rather so mix them together, as the hearts of hearers may be deeply affected with both; but first with their misery" (96). Since faith comes about only by first finding its expression in a conviction of and sorrow for sin, says Shepard, no one "can or will come by faith to Christ to take away his sins, unlesse he first see, be convicted of, and loaden with them" (5). Without a true sight and experience of sin, grace and redemption are without meaning.

As Shepard's expositions of the stages of regeneration proceed, they focus clearly yet with great subtlety on the central doctrines of the Puritan faith: justification, or the divine grace that initiates faith and forgiveness, generates and constitutes the ground of good works, and not the reverse; the soul's experience of being "reprobated never to see Gods face more" and its consequent mourning must preface any vision or apprehension of God's mercy (73); sin is an organic condition and so the act of conversion must see a "cutting off [of] the branch from the old stock" and an "ingrafting it into the new" if the old Adam is really to be exorcised (115); and to be "far from conviction" of the great work of regeneration is therefore to be "far from salvation" (22).

In the process of commenting on these and other Puritan doctrines and emphases, Shepard invokes many of the same images and metaphors he dramatizes so urgently and concretely in *The Sincere Convert.* The polarities of freedom and confinement recur, as do those of election and reprobation, stability and contingency, and union and separation. Doubt and anxiety still do mortal combat with faith and assurance. The sin of despair and the sin of presumption—that is, the error of "seizing" Christ too soon and assuming that one is saved, thereby most assuredly indicating that one is not—continue to be central to Shepard's concerns. Indeed, the danger that the wayfaring soul will remain outside of Christ is as imminent and threatening as ever: "the soule plyes both oares, though against wind and tide, and strives, and wrastles with his sinnes, and hopes one day to be better, and here he rests . . . [and its] being so sweet, rests in what he hath . . . and so hopes all will be well one day and so stayes here; although . . . it be without Christ . . . though he hath heard of him a thousand times" (127).

Yet even in this setting it is clear that Shepard's argument and vision are always moving toward an end incorporating a sense of reconciliation and resolution. The covenant of grace is his form of mediation and assurance and Christ is its center. Here sin may well lead to sorrow and humiliation to solace. Rather than the stern and avenging judge Luther imagined Christ to be prior to his conversion, Christ becomes for Shepard, as for Luther, at once mediator and merciful benefactor: "Remember his love to thee, that he came out of his Fathers bosome for thee, wept for thee, bled for thee, powred out his life, nay, his soule to death for thee, is now risen for thee, gone to heaven for thee, sits at Gods right hand, and rules over all the world for thee, makes intercession continually for thee, and at the end of the world will come again for thee, who hast loved him here, that thou mightest live for ever with him then" (345). Through Christ's intercession and sustained love "for thee," the Law prepares the way for the Gospel rather than for death. Finally, not only the soul's understanding but its will is transformed, for "in the Gospell not only divine truth is propounded to the mind to assent unto; but an infinite and eternall good is offered to the heart and will of man to embrace" (188).

This particular emphasis is crucial for Shepard, since faith is bound up with the heart and affections and not only with an intellectual understanding. It is experiential rather than notional. Further, since "a stubborn will like a stubborne heifer in the yoake galls and frets the soule" (152), true regeneration must result in the will's habit of charity. Given this end, writes Shepard, and given that "the kingdome of grace and glory is before you," how can the soul resist Christ's inviting voice? "Oh where are our hearts, if this call will not draw?" (245). Hearing this call, and acting in obedience to it, states Shepard, constitutes the very heart of faith: "Now for any to receive Christ, or come to Christ, before he is called, is presumption; to refuse Christ when called, is rebellion; to come and receive when called, is properly and formally Faith, and that which the Scripture stiles, the *obedience of Faith, Rom.* 1.5. And now Christ at this instant is fully and freely given, on Gods part, when really and freely come unto and taken on our part" (157).

In his dramatizations of Christ's voice calling the unbeliever to faith and the believer to an absolute sense of assurance, Shepard invokes the parables of the prodigal son and the "lively similitude" of the "*great Supper,* to which many were *invited*" (227). For the soul called to live in the salvation "the Lord hath undertaken in the Covenant of Grace," the reality of grace and assurance is "exceeding sweet" (167). In light of this sweetness, Christ's call becomes compelling in its beauty and love: "when thou hast been under the hedges, and in the high-wayes that lead to death, & didst never think of him, nor didst desire him, yet hee hath compelled thee to come in; hee hath made thee feel such an extream need of him, and made himselfe so exceeding sweet, that thou hast not been able to resist his love, but to cry out, Lord thou hast overcome me with mercy, I am not able to resist any more" (168). Shepard's solicitous tone indicates his emphasis on Christ's invitation of mercy, love, and forgiveness. In the soul's acceptance of this invitation, its anxiety and contingency are overcome and its identity and duration restored. Although the astonished soul may ask whether the Lord will "heale such a nature, take such a viper into his bosome" or "doe any thing for me," Shepard's response is clear: "This voice, *come unto me,* is one of the sweetest words that Christ can speak, or man can heare, full of Majesty, mercy, grace, and peace" (220). At the heart of this voice and word, says Shepard, is Christ's absolute grace in its willingness to pardon the soul's unworthiness: "I require nothing of thee else but *to come*" (220).

In *The Sincere Convert,* Shepard's most powerfully tactile imagery tends to concentrate on the soul's sense of pain and eternal loss. In *The Sound Believer,* it concentrates as profoundly on the soul's conviction and assurance that Christ has come to find and to save "that which was lost." In this light, however, Shepard would assent to Anne Bradstreet's claim: "The reason why Christians are so loath to exchange this world for a better is because they have more sense than faith: they see what they enjoy, they do but hope for that which is to come."[19] As Samuel Willard puts it, God's people are often so doubtful and discontent because "they do not as yet see clearly what they shall be," for only one who "hath felt it, can tell what it is to have the love of God shed abroad in his heart, and in his Soul to hear the sweet voice of Pardon, and promises of glory" and "to ly all night in the bosom of Christ, and have his left hand underneath his head, and his right hand imbracing of him." Outward and sensible signs of this glory, says Willard, "are but drops, and rivulets" which come in "little portions": "How glorious a thing then must it needs be to dwel at the fountain, and swim for ever in those bankles, and bottomless Ocean of Glory? How happy then are the dead in Christ, who are now seeing, tasting, knowing and experiencing these things?"[20]

As Shepard moves ultimately toward his description of the soul's glorification, he acknowledges precisely this tension between the desire for a "sensible" experience of grace and the necessity of apprehending it with the inner eye of faith. As with doubting Thomas, says Shepard, we wish to feel Christ "with our hands, and embrace him (as Mary did) with our arms" after he has "come down from heaven thus unto us" in order that we might believe (176). Yet despite our inability in this life to come to Christ with our bodies, insists Shepard, "the soule can goe to him, the heart can bee with him, as the eye can see a 1000 miles off, and receive the species or image of the things it sees into it, so the soule inlightened by faith, can see Christ a farre off, it can long for, choose, and rest upon the Lord of life, and receive the lively image of Christ's glory . . . in it" (176). The soul's relationship with Christ in fact may be closer than a purely bodily one, for many people physically touched Christ who were not ultimately united to him. If the soul departs from sin and rests in Christ, "this makes you nearer to him, then if your soules were under his wing in the highest heavens." Here Shepard again invokes the image of the sea voyage so biblical and allegorical in its resonance and so closely tied to his own literal experience of journeying and pilgrimage:

> The poore Sea-man when hee is neare dangerous shores, when he cannot goe down to the depth of the Sea to fasten his ship, yet if hee can cast his anchor twenty or forty fathoms deep, and if that holds, this quiets him in the sorest stormes; when we are tossed and cannot come to Christ with our bodily presence, yet if our soules can come, if our faith our anchor can reach him, and knit us to him, this should exceedingly comfort our hearts. (176–77)

In his descriptions of the soul "knit" to Christ in glory, Shepard overcomes the duality and tensions between body and spirit that mark one strain in Christian thought and celebrates their coalescence. In heaven, he writes, the angels "will love you and comfort you, and rejoyce with you, and speake of the great things the Lord hath done for you, as they did on earth to the Shepherds" (322). The resurrected body will be powerful and strong and "able to beare the weight of glory" (317). Christ's "blessed bosome of love" will open fully to the soul, and "never was husband and loving wife so familiar one with another, as the Lord Jesus will bee (not carnally and in an earthly manner) but, in a most heavenly, glorious, yet gracious manner with all his Saints" (322). In the soul's glorification, concludes Shepard, all personal and communal prayers will receive "a full answer": the "blessing of God which you sought for, and wept for, and suffered for here, you shall then see all answered" (319–20). The souls' musical "strings shall be then raised up to the highest strains of sweet melody and glory" (323) and any "darke vision of God" the earthly soul might have experienced will be replaced by Christ's merciful and ravishing love for the soul.

Despite Shepard's reminder that Christ will not love the soul "carnally and in an earthly manner," it is clear that his images and analogies are rooted in life, experience, and the desire to coalesce the tactile and spiritual dimensions of the understanding and affections. His is not a Gnostic, abstract, and vaporous heaven but a sacramental one. As he invokes his concrete images of glorification resonant with literal and allegorical significance, he emphasizes that they are not "delusions and dreams which never feed, but ever leave the deceived soule hungry, but are realities & things indeed, which satiate the weary soule" (323). His words and images point to and embody "realities & things indeed," and in this setting of salvation, grace, and glory, it is significant that language will be communal, conversational, and tender. Christ's deeply loved saints will "sit downe with *Abraham, Isaac,* and *Jacob* in the Kingdome of God" as well as "all the children of Abraham": "and there we shall speake with them of the Lords wonders, of his Christ and Kingdome . . . and every sentence and word shall be milke and hony, sweeter than thy life now can be unto thee; we shall know, and love, and honour one another exceedingly" (321). In concentrating on and celebrating this vision of heavenly and familial communion, Shepard recalls the covenant of grace as it extends from Abraham through the children of Israel and the remnant of Christ's new dispensation. He also affirms the marriage between word and thing, idea and reality, and in the process invokes analogies of earthly love—parent and child, husband and wife—to anticipate and describe the love Christ shares with his saints.

By making God's transcendence concrete and sacramental—and by envisioning the individual soul in a communal and conversational setting—Shepard also confirms William F. Lynch's contention that the most basic form of the imagination is not the endless or infinite but the definite and specific. The heart and center of the religious and literary imagination, and of life itself, he argues, "must lie in the particular and limited image or thing": "The finite is given metaphysical form in the concept of *haecceitas,* the pure and absolute *thisness*-and-not-thatness which the great Scotus saw in all things; in the "inscape" which Hopkins, following in Scotus' footsteps, saw in everything; in the single farthing of the Gospel, which was the key to salvation; and in the little, sensible things which were the source of insight for St. Thomas."[21] Shepard's imagery and analogies dramatize the presence of the covenant that provides the mediation and intercession through which a transcendent God and his fallen yet chosen creatures are reconciled. By fulfilling the Law through the Gospel and by overcoming sin through the act of redemption, Christ allows the polarities of light and darkness, death and resurrection, to coalesce. For Shepard, the Cross embodies the bridging of the polarities of infinite transcendence and earthly limitation. As it does so, it consecrates the particularities of language and experience and assures their importance in the ultimate drama of salvation. Not the isolated and wrath-haunted soul, but Christ's mediating covenant of love, defines Shepard's final vision.

Chapter Five

Inward Liberty: Shepard and the Mediation of Christ

As Shepard clearly indicates in *The Sound Believer,* the mediating power of Christ in the covenant of grace brings to the soul's awareness the paradoxes of faith: the last shall be first, those who lose themselves will find their true identity, and the heart of Christian freedom rests in submission to Christ. To elucidate and emphasize this last point, Shepard wrote a treatise on *Subjection to Christ.* In a letter to a friend, later published as *Certain Select Cases Resolved,* Shepard discusses particular cases of conscience in light of the Puritan vision of law, grace, and the soul's freedom in Christ and stresses the importance of the practice of meditation in the believer's daily life. This habit of meditation Shepard strikingly exemplifies in his own *Journal,* in which his anxious struggles with doubt and assurance, condemnation and forgiveness, define his sense of his present and ultimate place in God's drama of salvation. Throughout these works, Christ's mediation becomes the sole and normative means through which the often-terrifying polarities of experience are reconciled, dim and fragmented though may be the individual's perception, understanding, and experience of that reconciliation in this fallen world.

Subjection to Christ

Shepard's *Subjection to Christ in all his Ordinances, and Appointments, The best means to preserve our Liberty* was published in 1652. Although it draws on the Puritan treatment of liberty in the context of the biblical governing forms of ancient Israel—a model that John Eliot in *The Christian Commonwealth* (1659) urged New England to imitate literally—the work is centered on the distinction between a false liberty which is in fact bondage and the real and abiding liberty found only in obedience to Christ. Both Luther and Calvin, convinced of man's utterly fallen state, denigrated the claims of those who defined man's will as radically free, and the Scholastics before them carefully distinguished between kinds and degrees of liberty. Shepard's starting point is to be found in the way John Winthrop marks the distinction between natural liberty—what man is by nature—and civil or federal liberty. The first, or the liberty simply to do as one wishes, "makes men grow more evil and in time to be worst than brute beasts." It is "a wild beast" and an enemy of peace, order, and goodness. But civil, federal, or moral liberty is rooted in the covenants between God and man and among men themselves. While the first form of liberty is incompatible with authority, the second willingly submits to Christ's authority and that of his ministers and magistrates. It is, says Winthrop, a liberty to do "that only which is good, just, and honest." This liberty, at once analogous to and rooted in Christ's liberating freedom, is beautiful in its willing submission to Christ's loving authority:

> Such is the liberty of the church under the authority of Christ, her king and husband; his yoke is so easy and sweet to her as a bride's ornaments; and if through frowardness or wantonness . . . she shake it off at any time, she is at no rest in her spirit until she take it up again; and whether her lord smiles upon her and embraceth her in his arms, or whether he frowns or rebukes, or smites her, she apprehends the sweetness of his love in all, and is refreshed, supported, and instructed by every such dispensation of his authority over her.[1]

The world's kingdoms, insists Shepard, are ruled by chains and whips as they exercise their calling of raw power. But "the inward kingdom of God & government of Christ in the soul" provide a royal form of authority based on a gracious condescension: "There are mighty boisterous distempers, but the Lord when he comes in his Kingdome to sit upon the royall throne of the hearts of his people, now they flie: and this is the inward Kingdom of Christ, like a poore Subject pardoned and received to favour, he is before the face of the Prince continually attending on him."[2] This inner kingdom of trust and mercy, states Shepard, is antithetical to Satan's kingdom, and the conflict between them constitutes the heart of political history and the soul's drama: "As Satan hath an inward kingdome in the hearts of those that are without, so the Lord Jesus hath an inward kingdome in the hearts of all his Saints" (31). Inevitably, the soul must choose between the antithetical poles of Christ's "very spiritual, little seen" kingdom and Satan's: "You must be either under Christs yoke, or Satans and sins . . . as *Joshua* said, so say I to you; *Choose you whom you will serve*" (143).

In his discussion of the soul's real liberty and its need to repudiate false visions of freedom and power, Shepard invokes empirical and historical settings as they exemplify a sense of divine communality or selfish conflict: Geneva, Germany, Sweden, Egypt, and other countries and cities. By reflecting harmony or disorder, each place becomes a symbolic participant in the biblical and Augustinian drama of the two kingdoms or cities: the New Jerusalem and Babylon, the City of God and the City of Dis. In order for New England to usher in the Kingdom of God, and to have Christ's person and authority as the proper object of its love, it must keep its civil and church covenant with God "mediately" and consistently, for "the Lord never did receive any people to himself from the beginning of the world to this day, but he hath done it by some Covenant: Nor never any people took the Lord to be their God, but by some Covenant, they bound themselves to the Lord" (55). Christ will never break his covenant with the elect, says Shepard, but if New England and "whole *America* cast off" Christ's absolute power in church government, the derived power of the church, or the power of his ministers, its freedom will "fall to bondage."[3]

Throughout his discussions of the relationship between civil and religious authority and between conscience and law, Shepard continues to invoke the sustaining power of the covenant. He also notes that while the general estate of the church is democratic and popular, the government of the church, with Christ as "Mediator and Monarch," is hierarchical. To cast off the rulers Christ has appointed, he insists, "is to cast off Christ" (96). In an ultimate sense, Shepard's emphasis on the infinite value of the individual soul is radically democratic. He quotes approvingly Luther's description of the minister: "In regard of my person . . . I'le fall down before any [higher authority]; but in regard of the truth I administer, I look on the Kings of the earth as nits, nay dust" (103). Yet it is also certain that Shepard's vision, like the Puritan experiment in New England, did not champion democracy in the modern sense of the term.[4] While the liberty in which the Kingdom of God is rooted is dramatic and pervasive, the political and religious order necessitates the authority of magistrates and ministers. As Winthrop and Shepard agree, such authority enhances communal and individual liberty rather than subverting it.

In the process of commenting on civil and ecclesiastical structures and the dialectic between them in light of God's covenants, Shepard incessantly returns to the drama of the individual soul and the covenant of grace. He exhorts the soul not to fear presumption by accepting Christ: "Take heed, you refuse not so great salvation" (148). Christ's "chain" as it touches "the most tender place of conscience" is not a chain of bondage but of "liberty, and mercy, and love: Come and receive, not a Kingdome; but Christ, Peace, pardon, and grace freely; which may draw the heart, as it will at the great and last day" (148). Christ draws the soul to himself and helps to prepare the heart for the work of salvation. In citing Canticles, or the Song of Solomon, Shepard invokes the powerful and allegorical relationship of love between Christ and the church and between Christ and the individual believer. In that relationship, Christ is "the only crown and Joy of the soul, when the least look of love to a castaway is more sweet than kingdoms, ay and much more, that's love itself" (36).

The inward and mystical kingdom of real liberty for Shepard consists in submission to Christ and the authority of his mediating church and covenant. The soul's hope is to be "under the government of the kingdome of God." Yet this hope may not be well-founded, as Shepard indicates in a passage culminating with a striking image: "But now on the contrary if thou canst be content to receive the ordinances of Christ, and that is all, and the Lord never gave thee a heart to close with Christ himself, it's a strange thing to thee, that which is the main thing, the Diamond in the Ring of the Gospel" (37). This diamond in the Gospel's ring is the regenerate heart which comes as Christ's free gift. But for the soul to discern whether this gift is its own—whether it is of the elect in Christ's liberty-bearing covenant—demands introspection and the "private duties" of "Prayer, Meditation, Reading, and daily Examination of a mans own heart" (92). In order to know whether the glory of angels and the wonderment of heaven really have become part of the soul's experience, Shepard insists, the heart and conscience must undergo the most rigorous scrutiny: "Now beloved when the soul does thus receive the Lord, the kingdome of God is come to that soul; and therefore try and examine, is it thus with you? or hath the Lord begun to deal thus with thee?" (37). The authenticity of the soul's freedom through Christ's mediation must be tried and tested by self-consciousness, inward experience, and self-examination of relentless honesty in light of the normative truths of Christ and Scripture.

Certain Select Cases Resolved

The friend to whom Shepard wrote the pastoral letter published in 1648 as *Certain Select Cases Resolved* clearly was experiencing such self-examination, with its attendant doubts and anxieties. Shepard seems to have originally composed the letter while in hiding in England in 1635, after his first abortive attempt to sail to New England and before his approaching and ultimately successful voyage. In a prayer that God will bring his faithful voyagers over the seas to the glorious setting of New England and somewhat ominous hope that his correspondent will be preserved from national sins and their subsequent "heavy plagues," Shepard again points up the sharp contrast between the Holy City and England, the oppressive Egypt, from whose sins and potential judgment and affliction this exodus must deliver them. The tone of *Select Cases* is marked by Shepard's obvious affection for his correspondent. Yet his treatment of these twelve "cases of conscience," individually and as a whole, also represents a deep and traditional Puritan concern with the complexities of the inner life of the spirit. In addressing such questions as how to distinguish the covenant of works from that of grace and how to resolve the anxieties of a troubled mind, as well as such doctrinal issues as the Trinity and the distinction between Arminian and Calvinist conceptions of grace, Shepard applies his deep learning and exhortations to his correspondent's conceptual understanding and personal will or affections.

When Luther argues that even the justified or regenerate soul is always and at once *justus et peccator,* regenerate and sinful, faithful and doubting, he formulates what would become a seminal Puritan assumption about human nature in the spiritual warfare of this life. The soul's response to this fact of its condition, when marked by guilt, anxiety, and fear, becomes known in moral theology from Cassian through the Scholastics to Luther as "scruples." In Puritan thought, the method and art of casuistry becomes the "treating" or resolving of particular scruples, or cases of conscience, through the invoking and applying of general moral principles. Since the Puritans, like Luther and Calvin, had been accused of advocating moral relativism by excluding human works, ethics, and merit from their central doctrine of justification by faith alone, Puritan casuistry represents one of their efforts to reconcile specific crises of conscience with absolute moral principles. Such Puritan divines as William Perkins in *Discourse of Conscience* (1597) and *Treatises of Cases of Conscience* (1606) and William Ames in *De Conscientia* (1632) write as casuists as they attempt to bind practical moral situations and problems to faith and to general moral judgments and laws.

The conscience, says Perkins, is part of the practical understanding. This active conscience, or "synteresis," for Ames and for the Puritan tradition, is simply the individual's judgment of himself in light of God's judgment of him. In attempting to address and assist these judgments in such practical matters as overcoming distractions and weariness in holy duties, discerning the true source of the spirit's movements in the heart, and understanding the nature of the covenants affecting the soul, Shepard uses an intense yet patient tone that clearly reflects his personal voice. Asked by his correspondent to cite Calvin on a particular point of doctrine, Shepard indicates that he has long since "read out of" Calvin though he respects him immensely. Seeking to differentiate the true promptings of the Holy Spirit from purely natural causes, Shepard stresses the need for religious faith to be "experimental," or experiential, but cites Ames's witty admonition that "Arminian universal grace (as they describe it) may be the effect of a good dinner sometimes."[5]

Whether delineating ways to distinguish grace from nature, insisting that tumultuous storms in the heart often signify the presence of grace far more clearly than the deceptive complacency of stagnating pools, or emphasizing that real grace inevitably makes the soul more humble and thankful, Shepard's appeal is to experience, to order, and to the Word. The real Spirit, in contrast to Satan, is known when it acts for God's ends; when its actions are sanctioned by that Scripture which is "inspired by the Holy Ghost, and that not only in the sum and substance of it, but to every word and sentence of it" (48); and when its actions come about in due time and season. Shepard's teleological arguments from natural law and ordinary providence have a Scholastic cast in their interpretation of the soul's nature and end. Yet at the heart of his argument and vision again reside Shepard's traditional Puritan doctrines and images: the contrasting covenants of works and grace and the need for the Law of condemnation to preface the mercy of grace; the soul's need to experience grace through regeneration rather than simply understanding it abstractly; and the crucial place of self-examination and mediation in apprehending the experience of Christ's redemptive love.

As in *The Sincere Convert* and *The Sound Believer,* Shepard's conception of the covenant of works or the "old Adam" stresses the soul's susceptibility to the Law's shadow and God's judgment: "The least sins or infirmities do break the first covenant of works: and hence you do not onely deserve, but are under the sentence of death, and curse of God, immediately after the least hairsbredth, swarving from the Law by the smallest sin, and most involuntary accidental infirmitie" (44). Bitterly afflicted and mourning like one condemned to execution, says Shepard, the awakened soul may seek salvation through good works. But only "Grace in the second Covenant" is able to reveal Christ and draw the soul to him, insists Shepard in citing Hebrews 7, and therefore the soul must earnestly long to "cleave unto Jesus Christ by fervent ardent desire." Only Christ can provide eternal water for the soul's thirst through his "eternal election" of his people (113). In dramatizing the soul's steps to God—and, simultaneously, God's descent to the soul—Shepard invokes the imagery of loneliness and union. Pondering the workings of justice and mercy, the soul "first turns his eyes inward, and makes him to see his is stark naught, and that he has not one dram of grace in him, who thought himself rich" (95). Humiliated and filled with the pain of loss, the soul pursues reformation through good works but is left "a desolate widdow, comfortless, and sorrowful" (90). Suffering from the knowledge that he cannot atone for violating the covenant of works, the soul recalls Christ's promises and experiences new hope.

For the elect soul, "the covenant of grace is absolute" (40), and through this mediating covenant Christ keeps his promises and provides the sure ground for the soul's renewal of hope. The soul's experience of Christ in the covenant of grace, Shepard emphasizes, does not result from understanding and argumentation alone but from an experiential encounter of the soul's affections with Christ's blood. This encounter has a divine source: "The Lord leave not me," asks Shepard, "nor any friend I have, to a naked Arminian illumination and perswasion" (138). To be sure, Christ uses moral and rational persuasions in preparing the heart for conversion. But remember, exhorts Shepard, that "it is not the bare meditation, or strength of reason or perswasion, that elicits such divine and noble acts in the heart and affection, but it is the bloud of Christ sprinkling these serious meditations, that makes them work such graces in the soul . . . which bloud is the salve, though argumentation is the cloth or leather to which it sticks, and by which it is applyed; but from such leather comes no vertue, all of it is from the bloud of Christ" (138).

The image of Christ's blood "sprinkling these serious meditations" crystallizes Shepard's emphasis on the importance of the practice of meditation as well as his tactile sense of the experience of grace. The soul tastes, enjoys, and is refreshed by the "hony-comb" (80) of Christ's sweetness. Informing and providing a setting for this experience is the act of mediation. Shepard exhorts the soul to "renew morning and evening by sad and solemn meditation, the sense of God's love to you in Christ" and his commandments "shall not be grievous to you" (132). When "the reason of meditation comes," he argues, "take it" as a "glorious ordinance of God" by setting "some time apart for it in a solemn manner every day, and that in conscience" (30). The religious and heavenly thoughts generated by meditation, Shepard insists, are "our friends" whom the soul should welcome: "Let them sup and lodge with you all night, and keep house every day" (28).

Even—or especially—in the most difficult moments of meditative introspection, says Shepard, the soul must remember the unconditional nature of Christ's promise of salvation: "The greatest sins cannot make a breach of Covenant between God and the soul that is once really (not rationally) wrapt up in the Covenant of grace" (40). No sin, no matter how profound, "can possibly break that knot and covenant which so firm and resolute love hath once knit" (40). The end of meditation is the soul's affective experience of Christ's love, and Shepard again uses the imagery of Canticles, with its language of mystical union, to dramatize the soul's union with Christ's love. In the threefold act of grace, the soul is "raised up by hope." Once it is raised, it "comes to Christ, which is faith, by vehement unutterable desire." Finally, in coming to Christ, the soul "embraceth Christ by love, and thus the match is made, and the everlasting knot is tied" (96). When grace descends to the soul through the mediating instrument of meditation, the desolate widow and Christ are wed and the soul's fragmented desolation discovers its true end and home.

Journal

In urging the soul to the persistent introspection and self-examination of meditation in the light of Scripture, the dialectic of Law and Gospel, Christ's reconciling love, and the reflectiveness of the heart and conscience, Shepard speaks from his own practice and experience. The queries he asks the soul to make—"Am I part of the kingdom? Has the Lord begun to deal thus with me?"—are those he asks of himself. The Puritan end in meditation, argues Louis L. Martz, is crystallized in Richard Baxter's culminating image: "You are oft asking, How shall I know that I am truly sanctified? Why, here is a mark that will not deceive you, if you can truly say that you are possessed of it; Even, a heart set upon Heaven."[6] To experience and sustain the piety and direction of such a heart is to sense the assurance of everlasting rest, says Baxter, and "to find our names among that number" of God's elect.[7] Throughout his *Journal,* Shepard seeks his own name and identity in the traditional setting of meditation.

Although a section of Shepard's *Journal,* edited by Thomas Prince, appeared in 1747 as part of a work titled *Three Valuable Pieces,* Michael McGiffert edited the first complete text in 1972. Grounded in the tradition of meditation and composed in the first half of the 1640s, the *Journal* continues Shepard's early practice of keeping a book of meditations in order to locate his intellect and will in their relationship to God's presence. Few external events and concrete settings appear in the *Journal.* While Shepard may indicate the time on which the meditation reflects—a day of fasting, a Sabbath morning—or name a particular place as a setting, he does not develop their physical or literal characteristics. There is little of Samuel Sewall or Sarah Kemble Knight in Shepard's reflections and meditations; even the proper names are few. Yet Shepard's empathy with his wife in childbirth, his concern for the children he will catechize, and his preoccupation with his congregation and with the New England churches as a whole serve to emphasize his humanity and his commitment to particular and communal relationships. Many of his most conscience-stricken and agonizing moments recur on the Sabbath not simply because of his inability to sustain his relationship to God but because of his apparent failure to reach and address the inmost needs of his congregation.

In light of Shepard's obvious and persistent awareness of his surroundings and the individuals and objects comprising his external world, it is clear that the *Journal* does not dwell on them because it centers its meditations on the inner dialectic of God and the soul. "I desire to know God and the soul," begins one of Augustine's dialogues in his *Soliloquies*. "Nothing more?" "Nothing whatever."[8] The first sentence of Calvin's *Institutes* echoes this point: "Nearly all the wisdom we possess, that is to say, true and sound wisdom, consists of two parts: the knowledge of God and of ourselves." Jonathan Edwards often states this same central truth. Yet self-knowledge and the knowledge of God are necessarily reciprocal, for the soul's knowledge and love of God cannot come about apart from its recognition of itself as fallen and dependent, and self-recognition is possible only in relationship to god's reality. As Calvin puts it in the 1560 French version of the *Institutes,* "In knowing God, each of us also knows himself."[9]

For Shepard, it is this reciprocal knowledge that is concrete and real. Indeed, the tradition of meditation in its Augustinian and later medieval forms as well as in its Ignatian and Reformed Protestant structures continually holds before it the vital place of the affective heart in its apprehension of grace.[10] As an act of memory, imagination, understanding, and will, writes Thomas Hooker, meditation constitutes *"a serious intention of the mind whereby wee come to search out the truth, and settle it effectually upon the heart."*[11] To be sure, meditation engages all of the soul's faculties. But ultimately it must allow the Word to "soak into the heart, so that our corruptions may be plucked up kindly by the Roots."[12] By invoking precisely the same distinction between abstraction and experience he makes so central to his other writings, Shepard emphasizes Hooker's focus on "the sense of the heart" in the soul's meditation and regeneration:

> I . . . saw a vast difference between knowing things by reason and discourse, and by faith or the spirit of faith. . . . A man's discourse about spiritual things is like philosophical discourse about the inward forms of things which they see not, yet see that they be. But by the light of the spirit of faith I see the thing presented as it is. I have seen a God by reason and never been amazed at God. I have seen God himself and have been ravished to behold him.[13]

Yet the process by which Shepard, like Pascal, moves from a purely philosophical understanding of God to an existential apprehension of him, and, further,, is "ravished" to behold him, necessitates a painful dialectic of doubt and faith, despair and hope, and loss and rediscovery. As Richard Baxter notes, "Nor doth Christ carry us to Heaven in a chair of security."[14] Shepard's *Journal* locates with anguished self-scrutiny its author's failings, inadequacies, and tormenting doubts. The mocking presence of "Satan's wound" (97) in Shepard's consciousness and actions subverts his desire to remain faithful to God and to his duties as husband, father, and minister. He is plagued by his sense of unworthiness, and while his heart is often "moved and melted" (88) by remorse, he returns inevitably to his sins. Even as he reflects on the Incarnation, he is profoundly conscious of his fallen and creaturely state. It is amazing, he states, that the Lord "hath humbled himself into my flesh . . . to make a near conjunction between himself and me, for we are joined to man who is flesh of our flesh sooner than with an angel or with God": "When the Devil comes to make a covenant he assumes the shape of a man. And here I saw that our union is first to the human nature and so to the divine, because the divine comes down into it that it may be a means of a conjunction to God and of God to the soul" (99). The astonishing fact of the Incarnation proclaims the great work of redemption. Yet it also accentuates man's natural sinfulness by contrast to the perfect Christ who assumes humanity's evils, suffers its burdens, and dies for its deliverance; God becomes man in Christ, but man remains hopelessly fallen in himself.

Despite the "chasm" between God and him, however, Shepard invokes Christ as mediator and the salvific power of the covenant of grace as the ultimate bridges between God and his finite and wounded creatures. Only through these means and the Scripture can the human face and God's face reflect each other. Without the covenant, "the Lord's face is hid and his spirit withdrawn" and "there is nothing but a deformity in all our actions, unlike God." But the grace of revelation and the covenant restores the soul's identity and once more makes analogy between the divine and human possible: "This favor of the Lord makes our souls like unto God and our actions like to him, when God's favor leaves this impression of himself" (217). As the presence of the covenant becomes stronger and the soul's likeness to Christ rather than separation from him is clear, says Shepard, the soul's gratitude is deep: "My heart began to be thankful for these sweet looks, and I did covenant by his grace to be only for him and to be tender of his name and glory above my own life, considering that in time past I had not been so" (181).

Shepard's acute consciousness of his daily struggle to live a renewed and holy life rooted in conversion and to avoid lapsing into the failures of "time past" is both striking and moving in its drama. As in Michael Wigglesworth's *Diary,* the struggling soul loses God only to regain him and then to take up the combat and struggle once more. The Puritan's inner world, in its contingeny and awesomeness, trembles. As Shepard says, "I saw how good it was to depart out of this world and to be with God, perfectly near him where no more shaking is or shall be" (84). This yearning for stability and permanence in the midst of life's turbulence also reflects a longing for union rather than isolation. In a dispirited moment, Shepard dramatizes this sense of loss and desire for union in the traditional imagery of the divine marriage: "I saw with sadness my widow-like separation and disunion from my Husband and my God, and that we two were now parted that had been nearer together once" (98).

The intensity of Shepard's marital imagery of separation and union, with its biblical and even apocalyptic resonances, finds striking expression in those meditations centered on the sacrament of the Lord's Supper. Just as Edward Taylor's *Gods Determinations* reflects Taylor's desire as a minister to exhort the members of his congregation to avoid the despair that accompanies the fear of presumption in the Eucharistic rite—that is, their fear and guilt that they might accept the Host in sin and bad faith and therefore "eat and drink unto damnation"—so do Shepard's meditations on the Lord's Supper reflect similarly dramatic concerns.[15] Believing himself unworthy, Shepard is reluctant to receive Christ's invitation; yet his resistance itself then appears proudly sinful. If Christ could appear to bless the sacrament, he reflects, he would certainly believe in its efficiacy. But he quickly answers himself: "Should I not believe Christ did give me my meat unless every day he did lay the cloth?" (112). When efficacious, the elements become "signs and seals" of Christ's presence and promise. Yet they also signify that "Christ by sacramental union was given to me" (112). Ultimately, writes Shepard of the Lord's Supper, "I saw the sacrament a seal" of God's grace and favor, "for I saw that the Lord did not give empty signs, but it was as if Christ was present" (181).

By his emphasis on Christ's not giving "empty signs," Shepard rejects the doctrine, associated with Zwingli and many later sects, that the Lord's Supper is a bare memorial rather than a mystical and participatory sharing in Christ's actual body and blood. Yet by his use of the phrase "as if" Christ were present, Shepard also seems to deny the doctrine of the Real Presence as Roman Catholicism, and, indeed, Luther affirmed it. For Luther, the Real Presence of Christ's body and blood as embodied in the bread and wine is a central doctrine, though the act of transubstantiation so important in Roman Catholic teaching Luther specifically denies. But the Puritans more closely follow Calvin's teaching, in which the Lord's Supper is a "visible sign and seal" of Christ's grace.[16] In a moment of doubt over the very nature of this sacrament, Shepard wonders "how Christ could be in the sacrament and yet remain in heaven": "And I saw that Christ in heaven might and did unite himself by his spirit so unto these seals as that thereby he did come to the sacrament and so come into the soul and so convey himself crucified spiritually yet ready to the soul and spirit. . . . The Lord I saw could present Christ crucified spiritually and give him to the soul" (172).

Yet in this same setting of Christ's spiritual crucifixion, Shepard returns to the mysterious simplicity of the bodily elements themselves: "I saw the Lord did seal up his love by such common things as bread and wine (1) because hereby he was and made himself more familiar with us; (2) because we are so childish and such babes that he seals by things best known unto us, shows us his love not by strange and wonderous works but by common and ordinary things, as also because these were most common throughout all the world" (172). In this consecration of the commonplace, Shepard indicates, the hidden God reveals himself and Christ's reconciling work of redemption invests the ordinary with the supernatural. Christ's perpetual commitment to "seal up his love" in the commonplace images—and realities—of bread and wine constitutes a repeated sanctification of the creaturely world through a divine rite and sacrament. In this setting, the soul is fully joined in mystery to the concretely actual and divinely supernatural. Externally, and internally as well for the suffering yet believing soul, the Lord's Supper embodies the historical events and spiritual experiences of the Nativity, Passion, and Resurrection. For Shepard and for all of God's chosen, a "heart set upon Heaven" must pass through, and be sanctified by, this paradoxically grace-charged and "ordinary" bread and wine. By grace and faith, these elements become what they are for the Middle Ages: the bread of angels. The awesome power of the Lord's Supper, for Shepard as for Edward Taylor, stems from its repeated offering of Christ's invitation to salvation and the reciprocal transformations to which the invitation points: the fallen soul made a regenerate participant in Christ's divinity and the common elements of daily experience become sacramental embodiments of a transcendent God.

In speaking of baptism, Luther might be speaking of the essential shape of Shepard's experience as he expresses it through the meditative exercises of the *Journal*. In this rite, says Luther, God forgives sin, provides deliverance from the Devil, and gives salvation to all who believe his promises. This forgiveness and deliverance is "continuing," he emphasizes, for "our sinful self with all its evil deeds and desires should be drowned through daily repentance," so that "day after day a new self should arise": "This life, therefore, is not righteousness but growth in righteousness, not health but healing, not being but becoming, not rest but exercise. We are not yet what we shall be, but we are growing toward it. The process is not yet finished, but it is going on. This is not the end, but it is the road. All does not yet gleam in glory, but all is being purified."[17] Despite the intensity of Shepard's doubts and anxieties—the world's darkness and his own constantly indicate that "all does not yet gleam in glory"—his consistent repentance and his attempts to discern and to remain in a state of grace through a heart prepared for and receptive to Christ's love are suffused by hope. His terror is as acute as Wigglesworth's, but his sense of assurance runs deeper.

In one meditation, Shepard contemplates in penitential fear and trembling the nature of God's wrath and wonders whether his own name is to be found among the number of God's elect. He then crystallizes in a simple and moving way his realization that God's justice and mercy are not equivalent polarities and prospects but that mercy's depths are inevitably offered to the believing soul—and that God's love is the most encompassing and overwhelming expression of his power: "Hence I considered when I come to Christ there is no wrath, justice to devour, but sweet love. Wrath there is for refusing him, not else. It was then objected, But is it not to the elect only? The Lord let me then see I had nothing to do with that but to look on this truth which is to them that come to him, that he would stand as a rock between that scorching sun and their souls." In looking on this truth, Shepard's heart, and not only his understanding, responds experientially and gratefully to God's offer of salvation:

> Hence my heart was sweetly ravished and began to long to die and think of being with him. And my heart said, Remember to comfort yourself thus when you lie on your sick-bed, to lie under this rock as in a hot day. If one saw a rock in a hot day and should say, That rock will cool [me only] if I be elected and God hath purposed it, and so keep off in fears: no, God hath purposed that one and the other shall be thus to all that come to them and are drawn by his love. (85–86)

It is telling that the responsiveness of Shepard's heart occurs in a spiritual landscape of graphic concreteness, and that within its dramatic setting the polarities of sickness and health, heat and coolness, and exclusion and welcoming are resolved by the mediating power of a divine, ultimate, and generously forgiving love.

Chapter Six

Parables of Mercy: The Persistence of Hope

In the intensely lyrical prose of his *Spiritual Canticle,* St. John of the Cross describes Christ's mercy and love toward the soul. Inflamed by his love, the heart of the soul responds until the marriage is consummated:

> In that sweet draught of God, wherein . . . the soul is immersed in God, it surrenders itself, most willingly and with great sweetness, to Him wholly, desiring to be wholly His and never again to have aught in itself that is alien from Him. God grants it, in the said union, the purity and the perfection which are necessary for this; for, inasmuch as He transforms the soul into Himself, He makes it to be wholly His and empties it of all that it possessed and that was alien from God. Wherefore the soul is indeed completely given up to God, reserving naught, not only according to its will, but also according to its works, even as God has given Himself freely to the soul. So these two wills are surrendered, satisfied and given up the one to the other, so that neither shall fail the other, as in the faithfulness and stability of a betrothal.[1]

It is precisely this betrothal Michael Wigglesworth seeks as he bemoans his "wretched backsliding heart" with its false love and affection "going awhoaring" after idols. Despite his infidelity, states Wigglesworth, his hope persists: "Will the Lord now again return and embrace me in the arms of his dearest love? will he fall upon my neck and kiss me? for he was pleased to give in some secret and silent evidence of his love."[2] For Samuel Willard, all God-seeking souls are happy to "steal a Sight" of Christ or "obtain a Kiss" from him. But eventually Christ's presence is withdrawn. Willard's contrast between the souls' desolation and their heavenly union with Christ extends and deepens the imagery of love and marriage. It was a dreary day, he says, as the souls sat solitary and "pin'd away with Love-Sickness," recognizing that "now and then a Visit" from Christ was as much as they could enjoy of "his more sensible Manifestations of himself to them": "But now they shall be lodged in his Bosom, and his Light never be beclouded from them more. They will not be interrupted Caresses which they shall have from him, but they shall constantly solace themselves in him. There will be no more Coyness on their parts, nor Anger on his, but the Delights which they shall enjoy, shall be both full and uninterrupted."[3]

Despite the arguments prevalent in the nineteenth and early twentieth century that Puritanism is devoid of the sensory imagery of love in its thought and prose, it is evident that the Puritan tradition inherits and willingly draws on the intensely rapturous love imagery and analogies of Catholic mysticism and devotional literature. In dramatizing the relationship between Christ and the soul, and between Christ and the church, Luther and Calvin continued to invoke this vision and language; indeed, Calvin in the *Institutes* appeals to St. Bernard's *Sermons on the Canticles* with a respect usually reserved for the writings of Augustine. Throughout his own writings, Shepard utilizes this traditional language of affection, love, and marriage and mystical union in order to accentuate Christ's mercy and eternal fidelity in the covenant of grace.

In two brief sermons, *The Saint's Jewel* and *The Soul's Invitation unto Jesus Christ,* Shepard invokes and sustains, often in parablelike form, the relationship of love between Christ and the soul. As always, the binary thread of polarities is present. But Shepard's major themes are repentance, grace, and reconciliation. *The Parable of the Ten Virgins,* Shepard's longest series of sermons, also centers on the mediation of Christ's love and takes a biblical parable for its controlling image and metaphor. As a series of sermons written over a five-year period and generated in part by the intense conflicts over Antinomianism, *The Parable of the Ten Virgins* explores Christ's charge to and love for his church as well as individual souls. The work is replete with images of divine justice and apocalyptic fear. Ultimately, however, its "prevailing tone," as John T. Frederick writes, is that of "gentleness and persuasion, of emphasis on God's love and mercy" and on "the love of Christ as God"[4]—and, indeed, on Christ as the divine bridegroom and husband whose eternal faithfulness and affections are at once paternal, maternal, and conjugal.

The Saint's Jewel

The Saint's Jewel and *The Soul's Invitation unto Jesus Christ* were published together in 1655.[5] The subtitle for *The Saint's Jewel*—

"Shewing How to apply the Promise"—emphasizes both the importance of God's promises to the soul and the soul's need to "apply" those promises through faith and experience. Samuel Willard makes a similar distinction and emphasis in speaking of Christ: "We now have but Pictures and Draughts of him, and these very imperfect. We now enjoy him in Promises, and by Faith. But it is another manner of thing to be in his Presence, sitting at his right Hand, gazing on him, and receiving at his own Hand, all the Good which was laid up in the Promises."[6] In stating that "God made many promises unto his people" and quoting 2 Peter 1:4, "Whereby are given to us exceeding great and precious promises," Shepard stresses the promise as a central vow in Christ's work of salvation: "I am come to you this day," Shepard proclaims, "not to set out unto you the excellency of wit or learning, or the creature: but the excellency of a naked promise" (208).

Shepard's doctrine in *The Saint's Jewel* appeals to the understanding by clarifying God's reasons for making promises: to provide an object for the souls' faith, grounds for their comfort, and means by which they might comfort one another. In appealing to the will and affections, Shepard asks the soul to consider for its comfort the great hope that God will "cast an eye of pity upon thee" and "bring you home to Christ" (221). This consolation as well as the habit of living by faith Shepard accentuates by dramatizng the soul's relationship to the promise in the form of an inner dialogue between faith and doubt, hope and despair. Informing this drama from the outset is the metaphor of familial love with its powerful images of maternal and paternal love and the individual soul as a waiting and hopeful child: "it is with faith as with a poore woman that hath a child, and hath nothing in the world to give it, she takes the child at her back and goeth from doore to doore, and what she getteth she giveth to the child; so faith takes the soul, and carrieth it to promise after promise, and what ever she findes there she gives it to the soule" (209).

As ever in Shepard's vision, the soul's journey is fearful. The polarities of God and Satan, heaven and hell, and salvation and damnation continually afflict its movement and identity: "As Gods children have their names written in Gods booke," says Shepard, "so you have your names written also, but it is in the blacke booke of Gods wrath." Further, "as Gods children have a mark set on their foreheads so there is a marke set on you, but it is a woefull one"

(218). For those apparently outside of God's promises and those who repudiate them, terror is the sole reality: "Give me leave to deale plainly, it is as if a man had but two pence in all the world, and he should goe and buy a halter with it, to hang himselfe; yea further, all that thou hast in this condition, is but as if thou shouldest twist a cord together to hang thy soule in hell" (219). While "God is very carefull to send his Angels for the godly," insists Shepard, "for the wicked, the devils stand ready at his bed-side to fetch him into hell as soon as his breath goeth out of his body" (221).

By invoking metaphors of sickness, suffering, and imminent death, Shepard generates a mood of pain and crisis. By emphasizing the soul's doubts and struggles, he also dramatizes, as does Thomas Hooker in *The Poor Doubting Christian,* how incessant are the uncertainties and anxieties afflicting the soul's attempt to seize on the promise and sustain the reality of faith. Yet this form of anguish also serves to stress the authenticity of mercy and hope. At the most vital moment of the soul's surgery, indicates Shepard, the eye of faith may be able to look to God for deliverance: "As Surgeons when they let a man['s] blood, bid him look another way, so when the devill letteth your blood, that is, holds you poring on your corruptions, look another way, I meane on God, and then you shall be safe from the devill, and the world, and your own corruptions" (224–25). By apprehending a particular promise—"lie a great while on some one, and wring and squeeze it by meditation upon it" (225–26), Shepard urges—sickness will lead to health, the devil to the physician, and the darkness of reprobation to repentance and salvation.

As he exhorts the soul to wait patiently for grace and faith, Shepard emphasizes that God dissolves the darkness of hatred by love, the illusion of false promises by "the best rhetorick" (223), and the terror of eternal separation from God by Christ's maternal love: "None can plucke thee out of Christs hands, neither sin nor devill; she were a cruell mother that would cast her child into the fire; Christ must doe so, if thou shouldest goe to hell; yea more, if that should be so, he should rend a member from himself, for he is thy head, and thou art one of his members" (214–15). By invoking the organic imagery of head and members and the familial image of mother and child, Shepard emphasizes the closeness between God and the soul rather than their infinite separation. In so doing, he anticipates Harriet Beecher Stowe's question as one of her characters, a boy, hears a minister pray over his dying father. The minister asks that "we may suitably realize the infinite distance between us, worms of the dust, and thy divine majesty." The boy then describes his father "as he lay with his bright, yearning, troubled eyes looking out into the misty shadows of the eternal world, and I saw him close them wearily, and open them again, with an expression of quiet endurance." In this dramatic and agonizing moment comes the question: "The infinite distance was a thing that he realized only too well; but who should tell him of an infinite *nearness* by which those who are far off are made nigh?"[7]

In dramatizing the soul's dialectic of doubt and faith, objections and answers, and despair and assurance, Shepard persistently returns to this "infinite nearness" between God and believer. Essential once again to this dramatization is the imagery of familial and especially parental love. Though the soul "canst but chatter," says Shepard, and "though others hearing thee, regard it not, yet God will say, let me heare thee, and as a father loves to heare his child prattle, though others regard it not, so God loveth to hear his children pray" (214). The outward signs of God's promises may sometimes not appear, Shepard indicates, but the soul should not be fearful, for "it may be God dealeth with thee in this, as a mother with her children, who takes away the victuals from the children for a while, and puts it into the cupbord, but afterwards she giveth it [to] them again": "So sometimes God taketh away these outward things, and locketh them up for a while in the cubbord, which is in the promise, and when he seeth it best for us, he giveth it to us again" (213).

Shepard's imagery of domesticity and parental love and fidelity reinforces the analogical relationship between God and the soul and encompasses the infinite distance between divinity and humanity by an infinite closeness. In our own time, Simone Weil invokes a similar image: "A little child who suddenly perceives that he has lost his mother in the street runs about, crying, in all directions; but he is wrong. If he had the sense and courage to stay where he is and wait, she would find him sooner. We must only wait and call out."[8] Thomas Hooker uses the motif of the journey to portray the momentarily hidden God revealed and the child comforted: "When the father is going on in his journey, if the child will not goe on, but stands gaping upon vanity, and when the father calls, he comes not, the only way is this, the father steps aside behind a bush, and then the child cries and cries, and if he gets his father againe, he forsakes all his trifles, and walks on more faster and more cheerfully with his father than ever."[9]

In dramatizing the most timeless and profound experience of comfort and consolation open to the individual, Shepard's invocation of paternal and maternal love makes clear that the act of being found will overcome lostness and abandonment and that returning home, and not external exile, constitutes the believing soul's true destination. Ultimately, Shepard's appeal is to the Holy Spirit as comforter in Christ's promise that "I will not leave you orphans." Even through the experience of the soul's fear of death, says Shepard, in which all joy and comfort seem to disappear, God's promise of ultimate consolation should move the will and affections and be as real, steadfast, and reassuring as one's parents and home:

> Thou mayest comfort thy self against [death], yea and make death it self a ground of comfort and joy to thy self. If a child be at board from his fathers house, though he be at play with his fellowes, yet if he see horse and man come to fetch him, he is glad, and leaves his play and companions to goe home to his father willingly: so here we are at board in the world, and we are at play, as it were, among the creatures, but when death comes, which is as horse and man, we should be willing to goe to our Fathers house, which is best of all. (215)

The Soul's Invitation

Just as Shepard's emphasis on familial love and reconciliation overcoming separation and exile marks the analogous human and divine drama of *The Saint's Jewel,* so his intensely powerful stress on Christ as the soul's suitor and bridegroom marks the setting and movement of *The Soul's Invitation unto Jesus Christ.*[10] Taking as his text Canticles 5:2, "Open unto me my sister, my love, my dove, my undefiled; for my head is filled with dew, and my locks with the drops of the night," Shepard delineates in a moving and lyrical way the fervor and intensity of Christ's love for the soul in the pastoral setting of a divine garden. With its overtones of Eden and intense imagery of love and marriage, *The Soul's Invitation* dramatizes Christ's love extending to and soliciting a response from the soul and the church. Traditional exegesis interprets Canticles as Christ's song to his beloved church sung in a literal and symbolic—and therefore powerfully allegorical—style and form. For Shepard, as for Thomas Hooker and later for Cotton Mather, there can be no doubt that the church and the individual soul are simultaneously the objects of Christ's attentiveness. This identification of church and soul so central to *The Parable of the Ten Virgins* remains vital here as well. As Shepard states, the loving utterances of Canticles are "spoken in the person of Christ to the Church, and so consequently to our poore soules" (228).

By using a dramatic setting and a dialogue between an imploring Christ and the soul in which Shepard's voice is often Christ's, Shepard heightens the intensity and drama of his narrative and echoes the compressed and dramatic form of the New Testament parables. A renewed interest in the form and significance of the parable has resulted in an awareness of the ways in which parables shatter the audience's conventional expectations, reverse its ordinary values and ways of seeing, and proclaim the advent of divinity into normal and daily experience.[11] Parables are stories, analogies, and comparisons. As Joseph A. Mazzeo notes, however, "the term analogy in religious scholastic thought designates the kind of relationship which obtains between God and the creation" and therefore the parable addresses a situation at once temporal and eternal, human and divine.[12] Such is the intensity of Shepard's use of forms resonant of the parable that *The Saint's Jewel, The Soul's Invitation,* and Shepard's attempt to serve as vehicle for the presence and claims of the divine voice in *The Parable of the Ten Virgins* all reflect Sallie McFague's argument that the language of parable is "a way of believing and living that initially seems ordinary, yet is so dislocated and rent from its usual context that if the parable 'works,' the spectators become participants, not because they want to necessarily or simply have 'gotten the point' but because they have, for the moment, 'lost control' or as the new hermeneuts say, 'been interpreted' ": "The secure, familiar everydayness of the story of their own lives has been torn apart; they have seen another story—the story of a mundane life like their own moving by a different 'logic,' and they begin to understand (not just by their heads) that another way of believing and living—another context or frame for their lives—might be a possibility *for them.*"[13]

In *The Soul's Invitation,* Shepard invites the listener and reader to prepare for conversion—a new and redemptive way of "believing and living"—through Christ's invitation of love and marriage. Inevitably, given the importance in Shepard's vision of the soul's knowledge of its terrifying insufficiency and loneliness without God,

Shepard delineates the apparently infinite distance between God and the church or soul. Further, he invokes his traditionally binary dramatization by emphasizing the either/or nature of the soul's eventual marriage: "If you will not match with Christ you must marry the devill, and . . . sin, and you must be a hag and a baud for the devill if you will not be a spouse for Christ, and if he set you to murther your selves, you must do it, if you be not married to Christ; if you will not goe double to heaven, you shall never goe single, you will be bedded shortly in the devils bed if you be not married to Christ" (239). Yet if Christ is your husband, says Shepard, "if you be married unto him, he will fetch you home erelong, however he may suffer you to tarry here a while with your friends" (239–40).

For the soul and the church, the single life, metaphorically speaking, is not an option: the only question is whether Christ or Satan is the marriage partner. Yet in the image of Christ as bridegroom ready to "fetch you home erelong" resides the heart of Shepard's doctrine and vision. Christ takes the initiative in wooing the soul by his grace, for he "doth drawe the soule into his ordinances . . . in his garden" (229). He reveals his innermost feelings to the soul in his profession of love, insists Shepard, and in the process transforms the world from a wilderness of curses, briars, and thorns to a beautiful and aromatic garden. He discharges the soul's debts; redeems its nature by assuming the sin and suffering of that nature; makes the soul "as beautiful as the wings of a dove" forever, for while "death slips our marriage knot, yet it doth not betweene Christ and the soule" (242); and reconciles the soul to all things divine and now familial: "If ye be matched to Christ, God is as much my Father as Christs: and as for Angels, and saints . . . his friends and kindred, they are all reconciled to thee" (243).

The soul's joy in this reconciliation, says Shepard, is absolute: "You are made for ever happy, happy that ever you were borne, happy that ever you saw him in his ordinances, and that ever he came to thee in the way of love . . . happy that ever he tooke delight in thee, and that your heart is come unto him, to close with him, and to be his for ever blessed; Man or woman, thou art in a heavenly condition already and shalt enjoy him for ever" (247). While this joy springs from the act of marriage itself, Shepard indicates, it is also inseparable from the soul's awareness of Christ's infinite condescension to it. Christ's royal birth, transcendent dignity, and absolute beauty place him infinitely higher than any human creature. Yet such is the depth and "speed," or intensity, of his love that he willingly journeys from heaven to earth. When a king sends for a picture of a princess who might become his bride, says Shepard, it signifies his possible marriage. But "when he goeth himself out of his own land into another, it is a sure sign he purposeth to marry, if otherwise things miscarry not": "so if christ had sit in heven, and never come out, but sent for our nature thither, is it not a plain demonstration he would marry us? but if he would leave heaven his owne land, if he would leave honour for basenesse, then it is a plain signe he would be a real speeder" (233).

Although marriage for the Puritans was no longer a sacrament in the traditional Roman Catholic sense, Shepard utilizes as fully as Edward Taylor the powerfully liturgical language of the marriage rite to provide a strongly sacramental dimension to Christ's marriage with the soul or church. His desire to express the mystery of the Incarnation is also clear in this setting, and Shepard invokes a tone of solemnity in pronouncing the vow by which Christ weds the worldly and human creature: "If thou consentest to match with Christ, he doth so with thee, and so I pronounce Christ and you married" (247). In uttering this vow, "Thou must have faith," says Shepard: "Plight me thy troth, saith God, avouch me to be thine . . . thou must have him for better for worse, never thinking of parting if once you be married unto him" (244). From this marriage, now sealed, graces like children will be born and "the Angels [will] attend continually upon the children of God, in every businesse they go about" (246). For Shepard, the church and soul, when able to realize Christ's promises experientially, are wed to God eternally through faith in Christ. The marriage covenant, like the covenant of grace, constitutes a sign, seal, and mystical union by which Christ's gracious condescension assures and reassures the anxious soul that love and mercy are stronger than death and that reconciliation, and not separation, has the final word.

The Parable of the Ten Virgins

In *The Parable of the Ten Virgins,* an extensive series of sermons he preached over the last half of the 1630s, Shepard at once confronts the political and religious crisis of Antinomianism and addresses in an intensely moving way the perennial concerns recurrent in his other works: the need for faith, God's justice and mercy as they engage the soul and church, and the mediating love of Christ in the covenant of grace. The ten virgins of the parable are for Shepard the churches of New England as well as the souls of his people. His tenor is often apocalpytic, as is that of the parable in Matthew 25: the kingdom of heaven is compared to ten virgins who take their lamps in awaiting the coming of the bridegroom. But when he appears, only the five who have brought oil for their lamps are able to go with him to the marriage feast; the door is shut on the others. The parable ends: "Afterwardes came also the other virgins, saying, Lord, Lord, open to us. But he answered, and said, Verely I say unto you, I knowe you not. Watche therefore: for ye knowe nether the day, nor the houre, when the Sonne of man wil come" (*GB*). Throughout *The Parable of the Ten Virgins,* the sense of apocalyptic judgment is clear. Yet ultimately, Shepard's emphasis is on an apocalyptic mercy rather than wrath: "Oh wait for this time when he shall Redeem, comfort, glorifie, free from all snares and sins. . . . O teach it [to] your Children; speak of it one Brother to another; some of you are poor and mourning, oh be comforted, 'tis for your sake Christ will come, and refresh, and wipe away your tears."[14]

Shepard's tone of ultimate hope becomes especially impressive in light of the anguish, disorder, and divisiveness of the Antinomian crisis in New England. The doctrinal issues—and specifically whether justification, or faith, necessitated the believer's subsequent sanctification, or good works in the order of salvation—were complex, as was the doctrinal position of John Cotton, one of the key figures in the controversy.[15] Yet so pervasive was the controversy in New England that John Winthrop noted that "it began to be as common here to distinguish between men, by being under a covenant of grace or a covenant of works, as in other countries between Protestants and Papists."[16]

When the doctrinal controversy is reduced to its most fundamental terms, it is clear that the real questions involve the ultimate nature and source of religious and moral authority. By denying the importance of sanctification in the work of salvation, the Puritans argued, Anne Hutchinson and her Antinomian followers repudiated the vital role of Law and ethics in favor of a subjective emotionalism they attributed to the immediate promptings of the Holy Spirit. Further, by asserting that God continued to reveal himself through new truths and propositions, the Antinomians seemed to invite anarchy and to subvert the completed and normative rule of Scripture. From the Puritan social and religious perspective, Antinomianism represented the annihilation of moral law, scriptural tradition, and the order and authority of the ministry and magistrates and the exaltation of a radically subjective individualism. In strong agreement with the Anglican Richard Hooker's judgment on similar sectarians—"When they and their Bibles were along together, what strange fantastical opinion soever at any time entered into their heads, their use was to think the Spirit taught it [to] them"—Shepard played a major role in the attempt to cleanse New England of the Antinomian scourge.[17] For without the moral law and sustained obedience to Christ, he repeatedly warned, there can be only chaos. As Bunyan's Christian retorts to Formalist and Hypocrisy, "I walk by the Rule of my Master, you walk by the rude working of your fancies."[18]

In *The Parable of the Ten Virgins,* Shepard's exegesis of the parable provides ample and even epic scope for his commentary on the wise and foolish virgins and on his traditional preoccupations and themes. Throughout his delineation of the soul's and church's preparation for Christ's coming, Christ's differentiation between true believer and hypocrite, the nature of Christ as bridegroom, and the Last Judgment itself, Shepard consistently invokes graphic and pungent imagery and often in an aphoristic form. To accept a hypocrite as a believer is to have "a wolf by the ears" (1.117). The soul's watchfulness is always a necessity: "A man that will needs to bed at noonday, before night comes, what deserves he but a cudgel? So he that will die before his night comes, and while 'tis light to see and work by" (1.102). The soul whose desires are never translated into actions is "like a Bird that lies in the nest, but its wings never grow, there it perisheth" (1.159). Those with a "fruitless Faith" which does not experience Christ remain in a state of futility: "And so their Faith like a bucket without a bottom, draws up nothing" (1.181).

As he treats the journeying soul and church as they pass through the polarities so central to the Puritan drama—grace and reprobation, light and darkness, illness and health, Christ and Satan—Shepard invokes Christ as spouse, prince, king, physician, bridegroom, and reconciler. For many, however, Christ's presence goes unrecognized because of the false and lulling security the world provides:

Ministers may preach, and every man sleep still, unless some awake and rouse up the rest (as some, when others are abed and fast asleep) that lye a dreaming: Some there be, that though Doomsday were to morrow, they would sleep; Oh therefore let me perswade some one or two to fall to his work, lest their security prove your undoing; therefore speak oft one to another, forsake not your assembling, visit one another, pray one for another, warning one another, that you may awake with the Lord one hour. (2.10)

At Christ's coming, all souls will move from an abstract understanding of the event to a dreamlike awareness of it to a real perception of its actual reality. As the event itself moves nearer, says Shepard, some will begin to apprehend it but others will not, for all are voyagers in name but not all are in fact:

Men that live on land, and love the smoak of their own chimneys, never look out to other coasts and countreys, or to a strange Land, but Sea-men that are bound for a Voyage, and have a Pilot with them that hath seen the coast, that's it they look for; so men that live in this world, and are well here, look not after Christ nor his coming, but they that have a Pilot, a Spirit to shew them, this day, this coast, and are bound for another world, they look out for this; they see it. (1.89)

Those who receive God's grace see the "coast" of salvation through faith and hope: "Faith entertains the promise as a faithful messenge[r]; and sees that his message is true. Hope runs out of doors and leaves it with Faith, and looks for the Lord himself" (1.89). This emphasis on the soul's faith and hope pervades *The Parable of the Ten Virgins* even when the tone of judgment and crisis is especially acute. Shepard's sense of God's tender mercies to the soul and church is sustained and moving: "Labor to see who it is that nurses you, guides you, tends you, leads you, teacheth you, lays you down, and takes you up, and let the works of Christ raise up your minds, to the thoughts of Christ in heaven, remembering thee in his Kingdom of glory, who might forget thee; and the poorer and smaller the mercy is, the more do thou wonder that he should therein be a servant unto thee" (2.133).

What makes possible the reality of such faith and hope and such a perception of God's mercies is Christ's constant love for the regenerate soul and church. As always in Shepard, communion with

Christ is the highest good and separation from him the most painful loss. "What it is to lose communion with Christ," Shepard states, "I cannot express it": "The Disciples were sad when he went away from them in his abasement, but for the Lord to leave thee, when in his glory, to stand afar off and see him go, never to see him more, when no tears shall ever prevail again; Therefore if thou hast been found out this day, confess and give glory to God, and let thine eyes be tears, that Christ would overcome and draw thy soul with love, and espouse thee to himself for ever" (1.21). As suitor, bridegroom, and husband, Christ seeks to bring the soul to its true home, for "when marriage comes, then he carries her to his own house, and now live they must together" eternally: "When the Disciples had Christs presence for a time, it was sweet; but when parting came, that was bitter; but here is no more parting with the Lord; to be in a Kings dominion where peace rules, when other places are slaughter-houses, and Golgotha's, tis good; but to be with the King, and ever with him, and to follow him where ever he goes, and to be familiar with him, this is wonderful" (2.112).

Given Shepard's traditional preoccupation with the purity of the visible church in New England, his resolution of the problem of separating sheep from goat, tares from wheat, and elect from reprobate is striking. He clearly exalts the importance of the New England experiment in holiness: "When the King, Laws, and Subjects of Heaven are here met together in the visible Church, here is now the Kingdom of Heaven" (1.5). Yet while the church and soul in the following image are "poor beggars," the question remains whether those beggars who set their hearts on Christ will in fact be the recipients of his favor and grace: "The glory of the world is a Kingdom, the glorious Diamond of that Kingdom is a Prince in his Glory; now for a poor Beggar to have an offer of love from the greatest Prince in the world, would it not tempt her? Would she not forsake her lovers, and set her heart on him?" (1.22). For Shepard, the vexing and ominous question is whether those churches and souls whose hearts are set on Christ are to be numbered among the wise or the foolish virgins. If the visible church is pure in faith, spirit, and structure, Christ will embrace it through his promise and covenant. If it is to be a *corpus mixtum,* plagued by hypocrites and disbelief, its end would seem far more precarious.

Yet in a section of his exegesis and commentary, "Shewing that there are Hypocrites in the best and purest Churches," Shepard clearly and unequivocally answers the charge that New England's churches claim to be utterly pure and free of hypocrites: "though if Hypocrites could be openly and Ecclesiastically discerned, they should not be received in, nor kept in, because matter fit to ruine a Church are not fit to make a Church: yet we say there will be Tares and Wheat, there will be chaff and corn, there will be wise and foolish Virgins, there will be good and bad mingled together in the Churches until the worlds end" (1.119). As Shepard elucidates this more traditional vision of the church, he makes clear that Christ and not human beings will provide the ultimate differentiation between elect and reprobate: "There are not, have not been any Churches in this life, but there will be wise and foolish, Tares and Wheat grow up together; not Virgins and Harlots, not openly prophane (it may be) or wicked and godly; No, but when all are Virgins in outward Profession, and Conversation, yet then some will be wise, and some foolish in the sight of Christ, (though not in the sight of man) and between these the Lord Jesus will make a separation at his coming" (2.192). Although those who "have visible right to Christ" should ideally and inevitably only be those who also "shall have Communion with Christ at his coming to judge the World," says Shepard, the ministry cannot be "so Eagle-eyed" as to equate with assurance its judgment and Christ's. Charity and not an excessive or overbearing exclusiveness in its criteria for membership must be the church's watchword.

While the churches must "do what they can for the Lord now" (2.197) and continue to guard against Satan and hypocrisy, the ultimate tenor and emphasis of *The Parable of the Ten Virgins* make the work a parable of mercy. It is telling that one of Shepard's segments is titled, "Of Gods compassion toward wise and foolish Virgins." This inclusive image does not undercut the persistence of Shepard's conviction of the terror of the final separation and judgment and his concern that the church remain vigilant in its standards for admission. But it does serve to indicate Shepard's sense of God's love as persistently soliciting the reluctant soul just as grace solicits an often reluctant nature. In the covenant of grace, Christ initiates his wooing of the soul and seeks to make himself irresistible: "Let a man believe in Christ, and accept the offer of Christ when he can; but he can never do it, untill has heart averse to Christ, and unbelieving, be drawn to the Lord Jesus; and that not violently only by terrour, but by stronger cords, even the cords of Love" (2.184).

Ultimately, believes Shepard, Christ's love is stronger than separation, death, and the resisting soul. Further, Christ's direction and goal are always clear: "When the love of Christ apprehends the soul effectually, it overcomes the soul by sence of love, and thereby draws the soul from the strong holds and bondage of sinne to Christ; wherever there is exceeding deare love of the one unto the other, it is winning, it's of an overcoming nature; and though Christ doth threaten, or terrifie his people sometimes, yet the end is love" (2.184).

The psychological immediacy, apocalyptic urgency, and ultimate vision of *The Parable of the Ten Virgins* point to grace overcoming nature and love overcoming the resistant church and soul. As in his other works, Shepard emphasizes Christ's fidelity to the individual and communal soul through the covenant of grace. Shepard's exhortations of repentance to the soul and church are as intensely eschatological as his vision of the final harmony between God and humanity, transcendence and the finite. Christ's love consecrates even the most resistant creatures. Despite the profound differences between Shepard and one of Harriet Beecher Stowe's minister-characters, her description of his favorite subject justly serves to describe the reconciling vision of mercy and hope at the heart of the afflictions, polarities, and dramatic movement within *The Parable of the Ten Virgins*: "The last golden age of Time, the Marriage-Supper of the Lamb, when the purified Earth, like a repentant Psyche, shall be restored to the long-lost favor of a celestial Bridegroom, and glorified saints and angels shall walk familiarly as wedding-guests among men."[19]

Chapter Seven

Shepard's Legacy and the Religious Imagination in American Literature

The religious culture of New England, writes Harriet Beecher Stowe, posed with "intense clearness" and with "the power of lacerating the nerves of the soul" the most profound questions of our experience. In this setting, "there was nothing between the soul and these austere and terrible problems; it was constantly and severely brought face to face with their infinite mystery."[1] While the self-consciousness of the soul in its confrontation with mystery and divinity could be excruciating, she argued, the Puritan imagination had about it a powerful integrity in persistently pointing to matters of ultimate significance. By 1838, Emerson observed that the creed of those Puritans who "found in the Christ of the Catholic Church and in the dogmas inherited from Rome, scope for their austere piety and their longings for civil freedom" was "passing away, and none arises in its room."[2] For all its defects, states Emerson, the Puritan vision embodied a religious and moral significance that nineteenth-century America was rapidly losing: "What greater calamity can fall upon a nation than the loss of worship? Then all things go to decay. Genius leaves the temple to haunt the senate or the market. Literature becomes frivolous. Science is cold. The eye of youth is not lighted by the hope of other worlds, and age is without honor. Society lives to trifles, and when men die we do not mention them."[3]

For Emerson, as for other nineteenth-century figures, this crisis of faith could not be separated from a crisis of language and moral imagination. The believers' journey, Shepard had written, is arduous and often bitter, but the "weight of glory" at its end is infinitely precious:

Therefore let sinne presse us downe and weary us out with wrastling with it; let Satan tempt, and cast his darts at us; let our drink be our teares day and night, and our meat gall and worm-wood; let us be shut up in choaking prisons, and cast out for dead in the streets, nay, upon dung-hills, and none to bury us; let us live alone as Pelicanes in the wildernesse, and be driven among wilde beastes into deserts; let us be scourged and disgraced, stoned, sawn asunder, and burned; let us live in sheep-skins, and goat-skins, destitute, afflicted, tormented . . . yet oh brethren, the time is not long, but when we are at the worst, and death ready to swallow us up, we shall cry out, Oh glory, glory, oh welcome glory.[4]

The power and intensity of Shepard's rhetoric and imagery are rooted in his faith: the efficacy of language and belief is indissoluble. The passage presupposes and speaks to a communal and very special form of journey—one Cotton Mather would later describe as "above what any other Story can pretend unto."[5] It addresses the polarities of exile and home, suffering and redemption, and points to the Kingdom of God as an individual and communal end. Further, it dramatizes the soul's pilgrimage in an intensely efficacious language that bears out Emerson's contention that while modern religious language had become pallid and abstract, the sermons of the Puritans are "strong, imaginative, fervid, & every word a cube of stone."[6]

The Puritan mind and imagination, and Shepard's particular voice, resonated throughout eighteenth- and nineteenth-century American thought and literature. Puritan piety, writes Perry Miller, "blazed most clearly and most fiercely in the person of Jonathan Edwards, but Emerson was illuminated . . . by its rays, and it smoldered in the recesses of Hawthorne's intuitions."[7] The religious vision of human experience in its dialectical relationship with a transcendent and ultimate reality constitutes a central and recurring theme in American culture. In Edwards, and later in Hawthorne, Emerson, Melville, and other writers, and even in the often-apocalyptic literature of our own time, this seminal vision is apparent. When Norman Mailer laments that our language has become euphemistic and amorphous, he echoes Emerson's conviction that it is because the religious vision that makes language and images vital has declined. With the exception of certain existentialists, Mailer argues, the religious tradition in modern America had become "oriented to the machine, and lukewarm in its enthusiasm for such notions as heaven, hell and the soul."[8]

The Puritan conception of experience and the ancient religious and theological traditions in which Puritanism is rooted and by which it is informed make their presence known in myriad ways in later American literature and thought. The symbolic and emblematic view of the natural world so dominant in the nineteenth century owes as much to this conception as it does to romanticism: "Nature in her teaching," writes Harriet Beecher Stowe, is a "tremendous and inexorable Calvinist."[9] The struggle of literary characters with the intense realities of doubt and faith and moral conscience is an essential feature of the American imagination, as are the sense of sin and guilt and the hope for love and redemption attendant upon such struggles. But from Edwards through Emerson to Melville and such writers as Mailer, John Updike, and Flannery O'Connor, and while drawing on several religious traditions—not simply Calvinist but Roman Catholic, Quaker, and Jewish—four preoccupations recur with special force: the attempt to recover an efficacious language linked to a vital faith; the vision of America as a special place and idea in a divine and cosmic drama; the conception of the national and individual soul seeking the Kingdom of God while contending with the polarities of God and Satan, light and darkness, and good and evil; and the drama of an apocalyptic quest for salvation—often unmediated by forms of intercession—in which the soul, like America, attempts to find, or to be receptive to, grace and a final restoration.

Shepard and Jonathan Edwards

As John E. Smith points out, "Edwards quoted more from Shepard than from any other writer."[10] In his *Treatise Concerning Religious Affections,* Edwards's descriptions of the important distinction between authentic religious experience as it is engendered by the illumination of divine grace and an abstract or "notional" experience directly echo similar descriptions in Shepard's writings. Further, his dramatizations of the soul's contingency in many of his sermons, including *Sinners in the Hands of an Angry God* and *Future Punishment of the Wicked,* bear strong resemblances to Shepard's tactile and sensory—and often terrifying—images in *The Sincere Convert.* Yet just as Shepard's imprecatory passages serve as prelude to his descriptions of divine peace and reconciliation for God's chosen souls, so Edwards's severe invocations of the terrors of the Law for the unregenerate serve to emphasize the joy of the redeemed: "You will not only find those spiritual comforts that Christ offers you to be of a surpassing sweetness for the present, but they will be to your soul as the dawning light that shines more and more to the perfect day; and the issue of all will be your arrival in heaven, that land of rest, those regions of everlasting joy, where your peace and happiness will be perfect, without the least mixture of trouble or affliction, and never be interrupted nor have an end."[11] The movement and syntax of the sentence embody and point to the continuous grace and blessedness of heaven. If the soul's journey for Edwards is dangerous and marked by affliction, the soul itself, like its ultimate end, is of infinite value: "As the worm's dying and remaining in aurelia state, and then rising a glorious flying creature, represents the resurrection of a saint, so the spots of gold that are on the aurelia represent the preciousness of the dust of the saint, even while it remains in a state of death, being still united to Christ, and precious to him."[12]

Edwards's rhetoric, like Shepard's, is always imaginative, self-conscious, and in the sermons consistently addressed to the unregenerate and the doubting in the hope that they might be converted through the movement of the Holy Spirit. This preoccupation with the efficacy of language and images pervades all of Edwards's writings and consistently assumes that words are referential and charged with power and significance. Like Shepard's, Edwards's language is a "rhetoric of sensation" meant to impinge on the soul in ways at once tactile and salvific.

Throughout the wide and deep range of his philosophical discourses on the freedom of the will, the religious affections, and Christ's work in the history of redemption as well as in his elucidation of images, types, and analogies, Edwards is always conscious of the power of sin as well as of grace and of the Devil's reality in the course of common experience: "The serpent's charming of birds and other animals into their mouths, and the spider's taking and sucking the blood of the fly in his snare are lively representations of the Devil's catching our souls by his temptations."[13] The great work of conversion and transformation is arduous, as it is in Shepard's assessment, for Satan's power is intense. As Luther had argued, "The human will is, as it were, a beast between God and Satan.": "If God sits thereon, it wills and goes where God wills. . . . If Satan sits thereon, it wills and goes as Satan will. Nor is it in the power of its own will to choose, to which rider it will run, nor which it will seek; but the riders themselves contend, which shall have or hold it."[14]

For Edwards as for Shepard, this either/or vision of the soul's direction and ultimate destination applies to New England and America as well as to the individual. Shepard's *Parable of the Ten Virgins* had an immense influence on Edwards for many reasons, but one of them clearly is to be found in its apocalyptic dimension. Edwards's eschatological vision, both with respect to the individual soul and America as a covenanted and elect people, is deep and persistent: "My heart has been much on the advancement of Christ's kingdom in the world. . . . And my mind has been much entertained and delighted with the scripture promises and prophecies, which relate to the future glorious advancement of Christ's kingdom upon earth."[15] Yet while Thomas Paine's apocalyptic conception of America as an instrument of universal salvation often seems to presuppose the innocence and goodness of America's potential power—"We have it in our power to begin the world over again," he writes in the appendix to *Common Sense*—Edwards's conception is more ambivalent. To be sure, Edwards believed that America would be an original and seminal part of the apocalypse. Yet it is also possible to detect, as in the following passage, Edwards's concern that America's material power might usurp its spiritual uniqueness in God's cosmic drama. His tone here seems certain, but may be hopeful rather than confident: "The changing of the course of trade and the supplying of the world with its treasures from America is a type and forerunner of what is approaching in spiritual things, when the world shall be supplied with spiritual treasures from America."[16]

Given the potential for sin in the national as in the individual soul, and given the Puritan preoccupation with the logic of exclusive disjunction—if America is not celestial, it is Satanic, and, in Winthrop's words, worthy not of prayers but of curses—Edward's vision of America's redemptive and salvific possibilities necessarily is double-edged. All worldly power and goods, he writes, are "but scattered beams; but God is the sun. These are but streams; but God is the fountain. These are but drops; but God is the ocean": "Therefore it becomes us to make the seeking of our highest end and proper good, the whole work of our lives; to which we should subordinate all other concerns of life. Why should we labour for, or set our hearts on any thing else, but that which is our proper end, and true happiness?"[17] If this seeking for the Kingdom of Heaven is the individual's and nation's real pilgrimage and treasure, Edwards insists, God's gracious promise of salvation will be realized. But if the lure of earthly treasure and power dims this transcendent end and highest good, destruction will ensue. For the individual pilgrim and the covenanted people—the forerunners of the Americans Abraham Lincoln would one day call an "almost-chosen people"—the ultimate destination remained election or reprobation. In the far more technological setting of *Of a Fire on the Moon*—yet a setting resonant with the apocalyptic imagery of polarity and pilgrimage—Mailer poses this perennial question of purpose: "God was . . . at war with the Devil. . . . Did God voyage out for NASA, or was the Devil our line of sight to the stars?"[18]

Later Continuities

Throughout the nineteenth and into the twentieth century, America continued to envision itself and to be envisioned as the pivotal place and idea in a divine drama and struggle. If the individual soul is suspended between heaven and hell, grace and sin, and election and damnation, America's suspension was equally precarious. As a city upon a hill, America lived and moved with the eyes of God and the world on its covenanted saints. The drama of its experience constituted an elevated and magnified version of the drama of the individual soul. In this dramatic setting of conflict and polarity, Emerson's conception of man assumes new importance: "Man is not . . . ignominious baggage; but a stupendous antagonism, a dragging together of the poles of the Universe. . . . here they are, side by side, god and devil, mind and matter, king and conspirator, belt and spasm, riding . . . together in the eye and brain of every man."[19] This image of man as a "stupendous antagonism" in which "god and devil" clash for supremacy defined America as well, and Melville's Ahab, Twain's Connecticut Yankee, and every significant character in the American literature of this period articulated in some symbolic dimension an aspect of the American soul and pilgrimage.

In light of the rise of science, the "higher criticism" of the Bible, and a widespread skepticism toward religious tradition—Emerson himself resigned his Unitarian ministry because he could no longer celebrate the Lord's Supper in good faith and conviction—the disintegration of language's power and authority clearly was allied with the disintegration of faith. A bland and abstract faith necessitates an equally tepid language, and eventually words, states Emerson, "lose all power to stimulate the understanding or the affections."[20] The crisis resembles Mailer's description of the abstract jargon of the astronauts about to journey to the moon. For the return journey, Mailer wonders, "would the motor ignite, or did the moon have a curse?" But the astronauts speak only of "various contingencies" and "a wider variety of trajectory conditions." Yet they were "talking about not being able to join up, wandering through space, lost forever to life in that short eternity before they expired of hunger and thirst": "Small hint of that in these verbal formulations. . . . The heart of astronaut talk, like the heart of all bureaucratic talk, was a jargon which could be easily converted to computer programming, a language like Fortran or Cobol or Algol. Anti-dread formulations were the center of it, as if words like pills were there to suppress emotional symptoms."[21] The apparent absence of religious conviction makes impossible an efficacious language, and "meaning" and "purpose," in literature as in experience, diminish or disappear. Such a prospect is as hideous for Mailer as it had been for Emerson. In the same discussion in which he indicts the efficient blandness of much contemporary religious language, Mailer insists that "the final purpose of art is to intensify, even, when necessary, to exacerbate, the moral consciousness of people. . . . [when] one is using words, [he is invoking] a sense of moral commandments, moral strictures."[22]

Throughout the American tradition, the writers and prophets who have been able to reawaken the moral efficacy of the word—either by joining it again to the Word or by attempting, with or without a particular theological credo, to draw on some form of religious vision—have pierced "the rotten diction" of lukewarmness and falsity in order to "fasten words again to visible things" through image and symbol.[23] In the process, they continue to dramatize the movement of America and the individual soul as a purposeful symbolic journey or voyage of exploration in which self-knowledge, the knowledge of a symbolic natural world, and the knowledge of God's mystery are reciprocal and dominating concerns. On the journey, events are charged with dramatic meaning and significance. Although *Moby-Dick,* to which Mailer explicitly refers in *Fire on the Moon,* is the most striking example of such a journey, it is a pervasive metaphor in all the major American writers as it is in the Puritan tradition. The metaphor defines man as pilgrim and our common experience as teleological. The voyage's dramatic significance, again, is made more profound and apocalyptic by man's continual awareness of Satan as well as God, sin as well as romantic possibility, evil as well as good. In its various forms, the journey or voyage consistently embodies an apocalyptic and often Manichaean conflict between light and darkness, God and Devil.

For Emerson, especially in his early writings, America's "election," like that of the regenerate soul, necessitates an awareness of its divine mission and purpose. His exhortation echoes Paine's celebration of America's power to begin the world over again: "We must accept in the highest mind [our] transcendent destiny . . . [as] guides, redeemers and benefactors, obeying the Almighty effort and advancing on Chaos and the Dark."[24] There is nothing lukewarm in Emerson's affirmation, and its exultant tone marks a dominant strain in America's awareness of its own divine and transcendent meaning.

Yet given the either/or logic of exclusive disjunction, America throughout the nineteenth century could also be interpreted as Satanic and its journey destructive, especially when obedience to an "Almighty effort" seemed to become obedience to naked power or to the institution of slavery. In Twain's early writings, America's mission is benevolent; but his Yankee "saves" the past only by destroying the society he sets out to redeem, and *The Great Dark* describes a terrifying journey of nightmare and nihilism. Melville's Ahab becomes a destroyer. In "Prayer of Columbus," Whitman's Columbus is prophetic, but profoundly aware that his own madness may have given birth to his voyage. The corrosively ironic final epigraph in Twain's *Pudd'nhead Wilson*—"*October 12, the Discovery.* It was wonderful to find America, but it would have been more wonderful to miss it"—reflects the despair attending the discovery that America's apparent innocence belies its real corruption. Here slavery is the serpent in the American Eden. But more inclusively, America had betrayed its promise and its election could now only become its damnation. Dream was transformed into nightmare and paradise into hell. America's prayers, as Winthrop and Shepard had feared, had turned to curses and its saints had become devils. When Huck Finn must decide between turning Jim over to the authorities and thereby meeting the demands of American and, so he believes, divine law, or remaining loyal to him, he poses the conflict in dramatic, compelling, and ultimate terms: "I was a trembling, because I'd got to decide, forever, betwixt two things, and I knowed it."[25] In deciding for compassion, he believes his act to be an unpardonable sin. Society's reversal of the traditional polarities of heaven and hell, good and evil, virtue and sin leaves the inner moral conscience of the individual confused and haunted.

Like the soul in the Puritan order of salvation in which, as Harriet Beecher Stowe states, "all the draperies and accessories of religious ritual" had been "rigidly and unsparingly retrenched," many of the characters and narratives of later American literature confront the theme of a radical individualism bordering on and sometimes slipping into a desperate loneliness. The writings of Emerson, Hawthorne, Melville, Emily Dickinson, Stowe, Twain, and others are rooted in the images and ideas of religious tradition.[26] The isolation of so many characters in the American moral landscape—Dimmesdale, Young Goodman Brown, Ahab, Jay Gatsby, and so on—testifies to the darker side of such American ideals as self-reliance and radical freedom. It testifies as well to Melville's insistence that the Calvinist vision of original sin is a reality "from whose visitations, in some shape or other, no deeply thinking mind is always and wholly free."[27]

This darker dimension of American individualism is inseparable from America's expansive claims for autonomy. The American belief in self-reliance as seen in Paine's radically democratic vision and Emerson's early essays celebrate the sacred self, divinely unique in its goodness and power. While their critics argued that they were exalting man into God, they insisted that they were indicting the oppressive negations of the vast social machinery of modern life. Whatever their purpose, these prophetic figures came to see corporate religious forms, like all corporate political and economic structures, as suppressing the freedom of the individual self. As Tocqueville had noted, Americans remained largely unmoved by ceremonial and liturgical forms of worship. However the relation between God and the solitary soul came to be defined, it often seemed to exclude images of mediation and intercession—other people, a family, a church, the traditional saints, and all formal symbols of community. Emerson stated that the sudden experience of divinity had no examples and was "wholly strange and new" to each individual. Much later, one of Flannery O'Connor's characters expressed the hope for precisely this kind of conversion experience:

"When the Lord's call came, he wished it to be a voice from out of a clear and empty sky, the trumpet of the Lord God Almighty, untouched by any fleshly hand or breath."[28]

This vision is powerful but problematic. Shepard believed firmly in the experiential reality of grace and conversion. Yet his and the Puritan conception of the unmediated soul apprehending the workings of grace existed in tension with the church's corporate life and the salvific efficacy of the sacraments; Goodman Brown's repudiation of such corporate forms of fidelity makes him as demon-ridden in the Puritan world as in Hawthorne's. A belief in a transcendent God whose commands exist entirely independently of a socially covenanted and corporate faith may result not in peace but in a schizophrenic sense of conflicting polarities in which faith gives way to despair and God to the devil. Without mediation or intercession between divinity and the soul, solitude may disintegrate into spiritual pride or excruciating loneliness. Democracy's potential curse, wrote Tocqueville, and one inherent in the extreme forms of the Puritan experience, was its fragmentation of the bonds of community and its dangerous tendency to confine each heart in solitude.

In later American literature, this radical dualism between corporate forms and the individual intensifies, as when Mailer uses the dramatic and even apocalyptic language of polarity: "Any man or woman who was devoutly Christian and worked for the American Corporation had been caught in an unseen vise whose pressure could split their mind from their soul. For the center of Christianity was a mystery, a son of God, and the center of the corporation was a detestation of mystery, a worship of technology. Nothing was more intrinsically opposed to technology than the bleeding heart of Christ."[29] These conflicts resonate deeply in the American imagination. Neither a faith in American innocence nor in the saving power of nature, sacramental though it may seem to Emerson as a sacred image of Christ—"The aspect of nature is devout. Like the figure of Jesus, she stands with bended head, and hands folded upon the breast"—overcomes the dramatic force of the polarities.[30]

In Steinbeck's *The Grapes of Wrath* and Mailer's *Of a Fire on the Moon,* works marked by apocalyptic imagery, deep polarities, and searches for a mystical and transcendent kingdom, the sense of resolution differs but their dramatized journeys share real affinities. Mailer's conception of space is metaphysical and awe-inspired; Steinbeck's landscapes in Oklahoma and California are ultimately biblical and moral. The drama of the journeys they portray echoes the religious tradition Shepard embodies even as the desert and the infinity of space provide the literal and moral settings against which the drama unfolds. The essential questions—To and for what end does America engage its pilgrimage? Will human suffering finally be redeemed? With what Power has our covenant been made?—persist.

Mailer's use of the either/or language of the Puritan and existential imagination is relentless: "God or Devil at the helm—that was the question behind the trip."[31] He cannot call the ground after the Apollo 11 lift-off "hallowed," for he is not certain whether "the Space Program was the noblest expression of the Twentieth Century or the quintessential statement of our fundamental insanity."[32] Further, "For all he knew, Apollo-Saturn was still a child of the Devil. Yet if it was, then . . . the Devil was beautiful indeed. Or rather, was the Devil so beautiful because all of {us} were nothing but devils {ourselves}. For the notion that man voyaged out to fulfill the desire of God was either the heart of the vision, or anathema to that true angel in Heaven they would violate by the fires of their ascent."[33]

Mailer's language consistently invokes the Book of Revelation; Neil Armstrong states to puzzled reporters that the voyage must be made because of the nature of man's "deep inner soul";[34] and Buzz Aldrin, "a traditionalist with a faith that never seemed to alter,"[35] celebrates Holy Communion on the moon. To Mailer, preoccupied with the warring polarities in man's nature and America's soul, and committed to Emerson's definition of man as a "stupendous antagonism," Armstrong's conception of the voyage as the quintessential statement of man's soul could only raise once more—and with renewed intensity—the ultimate question of the voyage's real purpose and end: good or evil, God or Devil.

Armstrong seemed to have "such huge respect for words that they were like tangible omens and portents."[36] Yet his sense of the power and efficacy of the word, like his smile, might reflect Armstrong's innocence or his diabolical nature: "He could be an angel, he could be the town's devil. Who knew? You could not penetrate the flash of the smile—all of America's bounty was in it."[37] It is in light of Armstrong's representative image and America's "bounty" of innocence or evil, benevolent or destructive power, that Mailer's concluding description of the returned Armstrong—and America—must be seen:

It had ended. It was done. Armstrong's face looked remarkable. Never as at this hour . . . had it had so much of the shriven and scourged look of that breakfast food face which smiles in innocence at us from every billboard. A truly American saint. Of course, the Devil has power to assume a pleasing shape. . . . It had been a moment to suggest that in the mysteries of Armstrong's makeup, there might be a bona-fide devil in one soul if a saint in the other—assume he was twin-souled, yes.[38]

Like America, Armstrong is twin-souled—angel and devil, good and evil—and their polarities and antagonisms are made still more complex by Satan's power to assume the shape of goodness. As "heroes or monsters," the astronauts "were out to savage or save the rest of the world, and were they God's intended?"[39] Mailer does not resolve through an easy synthesis the ultimate questions he poses. But by insisting on the intermixed presence of good and evil, grace and sin, and light and darkness in the individual and national soul, he reaffirms the moral and religious significance of this apocalyptic voyage. The "two kingdoms" of God and Satan are not resolved into a final harmony, but their reality and conflict remain compelling.

Although Steinbeck's dramatized journey of the "Okies" seeking the Promised Land of justice and fruition remains rooted to the earth rather than ascending to the heavens, it bears out as does *Fire on the Moon* the ancient contention that all authentic spiritual journeys must be undertaken within ourselves (*intra nos*), outside ourselves (*extra nos*), and beyond and above ourselves (*supra nos*). Steinbeck takes his title from the Book of Revelation, in which God's judgment confronts humanity: "And another angel came out of the temple, crying with a loud voice to him that sat on the cloud, Thrust in thy sickle, and reap: for the time is come for thee to reap: for the harvest of the earth is ripe. And he . . . thrust in his sickle on the earth, and the earth was reaped": "And another angel came out . . . and cried with a loud cry to him that had the sharp sickle, saying, Thrust in thy sharp sickle, and gather the clusters of the vine of the earth; for her grapes are fully ripe. And the angel thrust in his sickle into the earth, and gathered the vine of the earth, and cast it into the great winepress of the wrath of God" (Rev. 14:15–16, 18–19; *AV*). As in *The Battle Hymn of the Republic,* the vision of earthly justice has a biblical, apocalyptic, and transcendent foundation.

The "prayers and curses" the Okies bestow on their literal and moral landscape cannot be shared by the banks and corporations that remain forever disconnected from the earth. In Steinbeck's vision, the American economic system of the 1930s desecrates the natural and moral world. But these dispossessed stay close to the land, praying for and cursing it in sweat, blood, and love. The setting of the natural world provides the backdrop against which their pilgrimage binds their individual lives into a community and even a kingdom: "The twenty families became one family," and "the children were the children of all. The loss of home became one loss, and the golden time in the West was one dream."[40]

Echoing Shepard's earlier description of the journeying faithful, the drama delineates the Okies bludgeoned by the forces of darkness. Drought, floods, human oppression, and the disintegration of families under the pressure of events afflict the individual and communal spirit. Yet the Exodus persists in the face of suffering, pain, and evil's corrosiveness. As Jacques Maritain notes in *Reflections on America,* the American awareness of evil is as deep as it is in Europe; even America's forced optimism and repressed anxiety reflect its knowledge of moral complexity and terror. Steinbeck's vision, like Mailer's and the Puritans', reinforces the conviction that the human condition and America's demand humility and contrition even in the midst of their outward sense of power and control. As strong as the currents of naturalism and technology have been in twentieth-century America, they deepen and intensity rather than repudiate the ultimate religious concerns remaining at their center.

As his narrative ends, Steinbeck links the biblical and apocalyptic vision of God's righteous anger toward injustice and exploitation to a mystical and immanent vision of divine love and mercy in which "all that lives is holy." Rose of Sharon, now an image of Christological love, whose biblical name is associated with Christ and with the Canticle of Canticles so central to Shepard's portrayal of Christ's love for the soul and church, suckles at her breast a starving old man. Their mystical and experiential union consummates Steinbeck's vision of suffering humanity, perpetually redeemed in time but still seeking an ultimate justice and peace. Finally, he indicates, the grapes of wrath will come to fruition in mercy. Evil will be subsumed in a larger redemption. Even in the face of hatred, conflict, and disintegration, the central fact and hope of existence is communal and transcendent love.

The shape of this promise and hope is part of the religious imagination and faith that Shepard's life and works express. To be sure, the irony so pervasive in modern literature would seem to subvert such images of hope and faith. Nonetheless, the patient search of exiled humanity for the Kingdom of Heaven—and its expectant waiting for its coming—constitutes a perennial and seminal religious dimension of America's national story. As wayfarers moving toward a state of salvation while afflicted by doubt and evil, the American pilgrims, and by extension all earthly pilgrims, measure the power of every secular kingdom in light of a divine order and vision. The suffering on the journey may seem futile, but it remains potentially redemptive.

Through his consecration of the biblical story of salvation and the power of the Word, and through his incessant self-examination and preoccupation with God's covenanted people, Shepard attempted to recover and restore the power of conversion both individually and communally.[41] Just as Mailer describes the voyage to the moon as "a venture which might help to disclose the nature of the Lord and the Lucifer who warred for us," so in Shepard's venture do we continue to recognize the persistent need to experience, to understand, and to dramatize the dialectic between God and the soul. The greatest dramas, argues Flannery O'Connor, inevitably "involve the salvation or loss of the soul. Where there is no belief in the soul, there is very little drama."[42] While contemporary skepticism would hold that drama is nothing more than projection and that the imagination does not reflect a supernatural world but creates it, the dramas and narratives of the soul's salvation or loss persist. With them also persists a faith, often torn by doubt, that word and image are in fact mimetic, that a seemingly profane world is indeed sacramental, and that salvation and not abandonment is meant to be humanity's ultimate condition. Shepard experienced as strongly as any contemporary seeker the power of doubt and the emptiness of what he calls "the dry and desolate heart."[43] Yet his affirmation of the greatest power of hope and faith and the plenitude of a divine and sacramental love—a love that does not deny pain and suffering but rather transforms and redeems them through the paradoxes of grace—constitutes the real center of his experience.

In giving resonance to this center through the intensity of his voice, with its own "best rhetorick" and images, Shepard exemplifies the power of the religious vision and moral claims to which his larger tradition points. That his voice so consistently expresses this vision and these claims in the form of urgent and dramatic narratives is telling. One commentator on narrative calls experience itself "an incipient story" because the act of narration is inherent in our being.[44] Given his own sermons, themselves testaments, it is clear that Shepard assents. By drawing on and referring to God's narrative of salvation as the sustained source and end of his own voice and life, Shepard seeks his own regeneration, his listeners', and that of the national soul. Only as language becomes proclamation and as faith's impassioned voice finds its response in others can the soul be restored. In that restoration, the sermon, confession, and narrative find their rightful generic and salvific place, related to yet encompassed by that divine plot "above what any other Story can pretend unto."

Notes and References

Key to Abbreviations

A *The Autobiography of Thomas Shepard*
AV Authorized (King James) Version of the Bible
GB Geneva Bible

Chapter One

1. Augustine, *The City of God,* trans. Marcus Dods (New York: Random House, 1950), 34 (bk. 1.29).

2. Cited in Albert-Marie Schmidt, *Calvin and the Calvinistic Tradition,* trans. Ronald Wallace (New York: Harper, 1960), 169.

3. *The Sound Believer* (Edinburgh: Robert Bryson, 1645), 281.

4. *Autobiography,* in *God's Plot: The Paradoxes of Puritan Piety: Being the Autobiography and Journal of Thomas Shepard,* ed. Michael McGiffert (Amherst: University of Massachusetts Press, 1972), 37; hereafter cited in the text.

5. Jonathan Edwards, *The Christian Pilgrim,* in *Jonathan Edwards: Representative Selections,* ed. Clarence H. Faust and Thomas H. Johnson (New York: Hill & Wang, 1962), 135.

6. *Certain Select Cases Resolved* (London: M. Simmons for John Rothwell, 1648), 144.

7. See William Haller, *The Rise of Puritanism* (New York: Columbia University Press, 1938), and Michael Walzer, *The Revolution of the Saints: A Study in the Origins of Radical Politics* (Cambridge: Harvard University Press, 1965).

8. Richard Hooker, *Of the Laws of Ecclesiastical Polity,* 2 vols. (London: J. M. Dent, 1907), 1:132.

9. Perry Miller, *The New England Mind: The Seventeenth Century* (Boston: Beacon Press, 1961), 5.

10. "To the Reader," in *The Parable of the Ten Virgins* (London: John Rothwell, 1660).

11. *Theses Sabbaticae* (London: John Rothwell, 1649), 1.

12. Samuel Eliot Morison, "Master Thomas Shepard," in *Builders of the Bay Colony* (Boston: Houghton Mifflin, 1930), 132.

13. George Selement and Bruce Woolley, eds., *Thomas Shepard's Confessions,* in *Publications of the Colonial Society of Massachusetts* 58 (1981). See also Norman Pettit's review, *New England Quarterly* 55 (1982):596–603.

14. *A Defense of the Answer* (London: R. Cotes for Andrew Crooke, 1648), 10.

15. John A. Albro, *Life of Thomas Shepard,* in *Works of Thomas Shepard,* 3 vols. (Boston: Doctrinal Tract & Book Society, 1853), 1:172.

16. *The Diary of Michael Wigglesworth, 1653–1657,* ed. Edmund S. Morgan (New York: Harper, 1965), 6.

17. *The Sound Believer* (London: R. Dawlman, 1645), 182. All references to *The Sound Believer* are to this edition unless otherwise specified.

18. *Diary of Michael Wigglesworth,* 54.

19. Søren Kierkegaard, *Journals,* trans. and ed. Alexander Dru (New York: Oxford University Press, 1938), 376.

20. *Diary of Michael Wigglesworth,* 48.

21. The typological vision of experience as expressed in American thought and literature is explored in Bercovitch, Lowance, and others (see the selected bibliography below). In its form as a religiously symbolic way of interpreting the world in light of biblical prefiguration, typology has ancient Christian roots. For its place in and dramatization by Dante, see Charles S. Singleton, *Journey to Beatrice* (Cambridge: Harvard University Press, 1957). Eric Auerbach delineates this means of interpretation and way of seeing in "Figura," in *Scenes from the Drama of European Literature,* trans. Ralph Manheim (New York: Meridian, 1959).

22. Augustine, *Confessions,* trans. Edward B. Pusey (New York: Collier Books, 1966), 155 (bk. 10).

Chapter Two

1. Ernst Cassirer, *The Philosophy of the Enlightenment,* trans. Fritz C. A. Koelln and James P. Pettegrove (Boston: Beacon Press, 1965), 139.

2. *The Soul's Invitation unto Jesus Christ* (London: John Sweeting, 1655), 233.

3. *Reformed Confessions of the Sixteenth Century,* ed. Arthur C. Cochrane (Philadelphia: Westminster Press, 1966), 121.

4. Augustine, *Confessions,* 77 (bk. 5).

5. Ibid., 128.

6. Ibid., 131.

7. *Luther's Works,* ed. Jaroslav Pelikan and Helmut T. Lehmann, 55 vols. (Philadelphia: Fortress Press, 1960), 34:337.

8. Douglas Bush, *English Literature in the Earlier Seventeenth Century, 1600–1660* (Oxford: Clarendon Press, 1945), 297.

9. Cited in ibid., 310.

10. *Works of Martin Luther,* 6 vols. (Philadelphia: United Lutheran Publication House, 1915–32), 3:350.

11. *Of Ineffectual Hearing the Word* (London: John Rothwell, 1652), 155; hereafter cited in the text.

12. Augustine, *On Christian Doctrine,* trans. D. W. Robertson, Jr. (Indianapolis: Bobbs-Merrill, 1958), 136.

13. Tertullian, *On the Resurrection of the Flesh,* in *The Ante-Nicene Fathers: Translation of the Writings of the Fathers down to A.D. 325,* ed. Alexander Roberts and James Donaldson, 10 vols. (New York: Charles Scribner's Sons, 1885–97), 3:559.

14. Francis Bacon, *The Advancement of Learning,* ed. G. W. Kitchin (London: J. M. Dent, 1965), 146.

15. *Subjection to Christ in all his Ordinances, and Appointments, the best means to preserve our Liberty, Together with a Treatise of Ineffectual Hearing the Word* (London: John Rothwell, 1652).

16. Thomas Hooker, *The Saints Dignitie* (1651), cited in Babette May Levy, *Preaching in the First Half Century of New England History* (Hartford: American Society of Church History, 1945), 13.

17. John Calvin, *Institutes of the Christian Religion,* trans. Ford Lewis Battles and ed. John T.l McNeill, 2 vols. (Philadelphia: Westminster Press, 1960), 1.7.5.

18. Samuel Ward, *Baptismatis,* cited in E. Brooks Holifield, *The Covenant Sealed: The Development of Puritan Sacramental Theology in Old and New England, 1570–1720* (New Haven: Yale University Press, 1974), 82.

19. For an analysis of God as *mysterium tremendum* and the believer's experience of fear, trembling, and awe in the presence of the holy, see Rudolf Otto, *The Idea of the Holy,* trans. John W. Harvey (New York: Oxford University Press, 1958).

20. *The Sincere Convert* (London: Humphrey Blunden, 1641), 16; hereafter cited in the text.

21. Cited in Miller, *The New England Mind,* 138.

22. Martin Luther, *Epistle Sermon, Third Sunday After Easter,* in *A Compend of Luther's Theology,* ed. Hugh T. Kerr (Philadelphia: Westminster Press, 1943), 119.

23. Calvin, *Institutes,* 1.7.5.

24. Perry Miller, "From Edwards to Emerson," in *Errand into the Wilderness* (Cambridge, Mass.: Belknap Press of Harvard University Press, 1956), 185.

Chapter Three

1. David D. Hall, *The Antinomian Controversy, 1636–1638: A Documentary Portrait* (Middletown, Conn.: Wesleyan University Press, 1968), 13.

2. For a treatment of certain of these issues in relation to Shepard and his congregation, see the references in chapter 1, n. 13.

3. Susan Sontag, *Illness as Metaphor* (New York: Random House, 1979).

4. *New England's Lamentation* (London: George Miller, 1645), 2.

5. Cotton Mather, *Magnalia Christi Americana* (London: Thomas Parkhurst, 1702), 2.

6. *A Defense of the Answer,* 10.

7. Jean Onimus, *Albert Camus and Christianity,* trans. Emmett Parker (University, Alabama: University of Alabama Press, 1970), 61.

Chapter Four

1. John Bunyan, *Grace Abounding* (London: Dent, 1976), 67.

2. Jeremiah Burroughs, *Evil of Evils,* and Samuel Bolton, *True Bounds,* cited in *The Grace of Law: A Study in Puritan Theology,* by Ernest F. Kevan (London: Carey Kingsgate Press, 1964), 84.

3. Calvin, *Institutes,* 3.17.1.

4. Ibid., 3.17.

5. Kevan, *The Grace of Law,* 193.

6. Giles Firmin, "To the Reader," in *The Real Christian* (London: Dorman Newman, 1670).

7. Ibid., 214.

8. Ibid., 215.

9. Augustine, *Enarrationes in Psalmos (On the Psalms),* cited in *An Augustine Synthesis,* ed. Erich Przywara (New York: Harper, 1958), 425.

10. For an account of this process, see Edmund S. Morgan, *Visible Saints: The History of a Puritan Idea* (New York: New York University Press, 1963), chap. 3.

11. See Norman Pettit, *The Heart Prepared: Grace and Conversion in Puritan Spiritual Life* (New Haven: Yale University Press, 1966), and Kevan, *The Grace of Law.*

12. *Studies in Human Time,* trans. Elliott Coleman (Baltimore: Johns Hopkins University Press, 1956), 12.

13. Ibid., 11.

14. Ibid., 12.

15. *The Sound Believer,* 4; see also 313–28.

16. See Delbert R. Hillers, *Covenant: The History of a Biblical Idea* (Baltimore: Johns Hopkins Press, 1969); Miller, *The New England Mind,* bk. 4; and Holifield, *The Covenant Sealed.*

17. Samuel Willard, *A Compleat Body of Divinity* (Boston: B. Green and S. Kneeland for B. Eliot and D. Henchman, 1726), 238.

18. Ibid., 515.

19. Anne Bradstreet, *Meditations,* no. 13, cited in *The American Puritans: Their Prose and Poetry,* ed. Perry Miller (New York: Columbia University Press, 1982), 278.

20. Samuel Willard, *The Child's Portion* (1684), cited in *The Puritans,* ed. Perry Miller and Thomas H. Johnson, 2 vols. (New York: Harper, 1963), 1:371.

21. William F. Lynch, *Christ and Apollo* (New York: Sheed and Ward, 1960), 4–5.

Chapter Five

1. John Winthrop, "Speech to the General Court," in *The American Puritans,* ed. Miller, 92–93.

2. *Subjection to Christ,* 7–8.

3. Ibid., 53. Shepard defines as a "three-fold cord" which must not be broken Christ's absolute power in church government; Christ's derivative power in and through the church; and the power of Christ's ministry.

4. The estate of the church, says Shepard, is "Democratical" and "Popular" but its government is "Aristocratical" (*Subjection to Christ,* 96). For a consideration of early New England Puritanism and democracy, see Miller, "Thomas Hooker and the Democracy of Connecticut," in *Errand into the Wilderness,* 16–47. See also Clinton Rossiter, "Thomas Hooker," *New England Quarterly* 25 (1952):459–88, for a rejoinder to Miller's contention that the Puritan experiment was not democratic. Nathan O. Hatch, *The Sacred Cause of Liberty: Republican Thought and the Millennium in Revolutionary New England* (New Haven: Yale University Press, 1977), explores the political dimensions and implications of the New England religious vision for later revolutionary and apocalyptic thought in that culture.

5. *Certain Select Cases Resolved,* 156.

6. Cited in Louis L. Martz, *The Poetry of Meditation: A Study in English Religious Literature* (New Haven: Yale University Press, 1962), 163.

7. See ibid., 153–75.

8. Augustine, *Soliloquies,* 1.2.7; cited in Calvin, *Institutes,* 1:36, n. 3.

9. Ibid.

10. See Calvin, *Institutes;* Martz, *The Poetry of Meditation;* Pettit, *The Heart Prepared;* and Perry Miller's emphasis on the importance of "the sense of the heart" in Jonathan Edwards's writings.

11. Thomas Hooker, "Meditation," in *The Puritans,* ed. Miller and Johnson, 1:301.

12. Ibid., 1:304.

13. *Journal,* in *God's Plot,* ed. McGiffert, 136.

14. Richard Baxter, *The Saints' Everlasting Rest,* 9th ed. (London: F. Tyton and J. Underhill, 1662), 17.

15. For the twin dangers of despair and presumption in the soul's preparation for the Lord's Supper as well as the depth of Christ's invitation and assurance as Edward Taylor dramatizes these Puritan concerns, see Michael J. Colacurcio, "Gods Determinations Touching Half-Way Membership: Occasion and Audience in Edward Taylor," *American Literature* 39 (1967):298–314.

16. See Perry Miller, "The Puritan Theory of the Sacraments in Seventeenth-Century New England," *Catholic Historical Review* 22 (1937):409–25, and Holifield, *The Covenant Sealed.*

17. Luther, *Small Catechism.*

Chapter Six

1. St. John of the Cross, *Spiritual Canticle,* trans. and ed. E. Allison Peers (New York: Doubleday, 1961), 138.

2. *Diary of Michael Wigglesworth,* 13.

3. Willard, *A Compleat Body of Divinity,* 557.

4. John T. Frederick, "Literary Art in Thomas Shepard's *The Parable of the Ten Virgins,*" *Seventeenth-Century News* 26 (Spring 1968):6.

5. *The Saints Jewel, Shewing How to apply the Promise; And the Souls Invitation unto Jesus Christ* (London: John Sweeting, 1655).

6. Willard, *A Compleat Body of Divinity,* 557–58.

7. Harriet Beecher Stowe, *Oldtown Folks,* ed. Henry F. May (Cambridge: Harvard University Press, Belknap Press, 1966), 61.

8. Simone Weil, "Some Reflections on the Love of God," in *On Science, Necessity, and the Love of God,* ed. Richard Rees (London: Oxford University Press, 1968), 159.

9. Thomas Hooker, *The Soules Ingraffing* (1637), cited in Levy, *Preaching in the First Half Century of New England History,* 114.

10. See note 5 above.

11. See, for example, John Dominic Crossan, *The Dark Interval: Towards a Theology of Story* (Allen, Tex.: Argus Communications, 1975), and Sallie McFague, *Speaking in Parables: A Study in Metaphor and Theology* (Philadelphia: Fortess Press, 1973).

12. Joseph A. Mazzeo, *Medieval Cultural Tradition in Dante's Comedy* (Ithaca: Cornell University Press, 1960), 10.

13. McFague, *Speaking in Parables,* 78–79.

14. *The Parable of the Ten Virgins* (London: John Rothwell, 1660), 2.203. Since the work is divided into two major parts, the first number refers to the part of the work and the second to the page.

15. For a treatment of the controversy, including primary sources, see Hall, ed., *The Antinomian Controversy.*

16. Winthrop, *Journal,* cited in *The American Puritans,* ed. Miller, 53–54.

17. Richard Hooker, *Of the Laws of Ecclesiastical Polity,* ed. A. S. McGrade and Brian Vickers (New York: St. Martin's Press, 1975), 97.

18. Cited in Kevan, *The Grace of Law,* 195. For a useful context for this question, see chapter 6, "Christian Law-Keeping," in ibid., 195–223.

19. Harriet Beecher Stowe, *The Minister's Wooing* (Ridgewood, N.J.: Gregg Press, 1968), 115.

Chapter Seven

1. Stowe, *Oldtown Folks,* 72.
2. Emerson, "Divinity School Address," in *Selections from Ralph Waldo Emerson,* ed. Stephen E. Whicher (Boston: Houghton Mifflin, 1960), 111.
3. Ibid., 112.
4. *The Sound Believer* (Edinburgh: R. Bryson, 1645), 281.
5. Mather, *Magnalia Christi Americana,* 3.
6. *Journals and Miscellaneous Notebooks of Ralph Waldo Emerson,* ed. William H. Gilman and J. E. Parsons (Cambridge, Mass.: Belknap Press of Harvard University Press, 1970), 8:231.
7. Miller, *The New England Mind,* 5.
8. Norman Mailer, "Catholic and Protestant," in "The Hip and the Square," in *Advertisements for Myself* (New York: G. P. Putnam's Sons, 1959), 426.
9. Stowe, *Oldtown Folks,* 71.
10. Introduction to Jonathan Edwards's *Religious Affections,* ed. John E. Smith (New Haven: Yale University Press, 1959), 55.
11. Edwards, *The Peace Which Christ Gives,* in *Jonathan Edwards: Representative Selections,* 143.
12. Jonathan Edwards, *Images or Shadows of Divine Things,* ed. Perry Miller (Westport, Conn.: Greenwood Press, 1977), no. 144.
13. Ibid., no. 11.
14. Luther, *Bondage of the Will,* in *A Compend of Luther's Theology,* 90.
15. Edwards, *Personal Narrative,* in *Jonathan Edwards: Representative Selections,* 68.
16. Edwards, *Images or Shadows of Divine Things,* no. 147.
17. Edwards, *The Christian Pilgrim,* in *Jonathan Edwards: Representative Selections*, 131–32.
18. Norman Mailer. *Of a Fire on the Moon* (Boston: Little, Brown, 1970), 80.
19. Emerson, *Fate,* in *Selections from Ralph Waldo Emerson,* 340.
20. Emerson, *Nature,* in ibid., 33–34.
21. Mailer, *Of a Fire on the Moon,* 25.
22. Cited in Richard G. Stern, "Hip, Hell, and the Navigator: An Interview with Norman Mailer," in *Advertisements for Myself,* by Mailer, 384.
23. Emerson, *Nature,* in *Selections from Ralph Waldo Emerson,* 34.
24. Emerson, *Self-Reliance,* in ibid., 148.
25. Samuel Clemens, *Adventures of Huckleberry Finn,* ed. Sculley Bradley et al. (New York: W. W. Norton, 1977), 169 (chap. 21).
26. Besides the works by Lowance, Colacurcio, Shurr, and Bercovitch

included in the selected bibliography, see, for example, Charles H. Foster, *The Rungless Ladder: Harriet Beecher Stowe and New England Puritanism* (Durham, N.C.: Duke University Press, 1954); Lawrence Buell, *Literary Transcendentalism: Style and Vision in the American Renaissance* (Ithaca: Cornell University Press, 1973); Thomas Werge, "*Moby-Dick* and the Calvinist Tradition," *Studies in the Novel* 1 (Winter 1969); T. Walter Herbert, Jr., *Moby-Dick and Calvinism* (New Brunswick, N.J.: Rutgers University Press, 1977); and Rowland A. Sherrill, *The Prophetic Melville: Experience, Transcendence, and Tragedy* (Athens, Ga.: University of Georgia Press, 1979).

27. Melville, "Hawthorne and His Mosses," in *The Portable Melville*, ed. Jay Leyda (New York: Viking Press, 1961), 406.

28. Flannery O'Connor, *The Violent Bear It Away* (New York: Farrar, Straus & Cudahy, 1960)), 22.

29. Norman Mailer, *The Armies of the Night* (New York: New American Library, 1968), 211–12.

30. Emerson, *Nature*, in *Selections from Ralph Waldo Emerson*, 49.

31. Mailer, *Of a Fire on the Moon*, 456.

32. Ibid., 15.

33. Ibid., 103.

34. Ibid., 42.

35. Ibid., 338.

36. Ibid., 30.

37. Ibid.

38. Ibid., 454.

39. Ibid., 441.

40. John Steinbeck, *The Grapes of Wrath* (New York: Random House, 1939), 264 (chap. 17).

41. For a brief consideration of Shepard in light of conceptions of narrative, see Leopold Damrosch, Jr., *God's Plot and Man's Stories: Studies in the Fictional Imagination from Milton to Fielding* (Chicago: University of Chicago Press, 1985). Several of Damrosch's observations are illuminating, though his contentions that Shepard's universe is devoid of any sacramental presence and that Shepard himself is "a profoundly troubled personality in which health and sickness are utterly inseparable" (49) are problematic.

42. Flannery O'Connor, "Novelist and Believer," in *Religion and Modern Literature: Essays in Theory and Criticism*, ed. G. B. Tennyson and Edward E. Ericson, Jr. (Grand Rapids, Mich.: Eerdmans, 1975), 74.

43. *The Sound Believer*, 149.

44. Stephen Crites, "The Narrative Quality of Experience," *Journal of the American Academy of Religion* 39 (September 1971):297.

Selected Bibliography

PRIMARY SOURCES

John A. Albro's three-volume edition of Shepard's *Works* (Boston: Doctrinal Tract & Book Society, 1853), reprinted in 1967 (New York: AMS Press), is the standard edition. Albro often utilizes later editions of Shepard's writings, including those revised substantially in the process by Thomas Prince (see Michael McGiffert, "Introduction," below). For bibliographical information on Shepard's works, see Joseph Sabin, *Bibliotheca Americana* (1868–1936) and Charles Evans, *American Bibliography* (1903–59). Since the first and immediately subsequent editions of Shepard's writings were published in England, Donald A. Wing, *Short-Title Catalogue* (1945–51), is an indispensable source. A number of the less accessible primary sources have been or are being made available in microfilm and microprint. I have used the first editions of Shepard's works (cited below).

Autobiography. Edited by Nehemiah Adams. Boston: Pierce & Parker, 1832.

Autobiography. In *God's Plot: The Paradoxes of Puritan Piety. Being the Autobiography and Journal of Thomas Shepard,* edited by Michael McGiffert. Amherst: University of Massachusetts Press, 1972.

Certain Select Cases Resolved. London: M. Simmons for John Rothwell, 1648.

The Church-Membership of Children, and Their Right to Baptisme. Cambridge, Mass.: Samuel Green, 1663.

The Clear Sun-shine of the Gospel Breaking Forth upon the Indians in New-England. London: R. Cotes for John Bellamy, 1648.

The Day-Breaking, if not the Sun-Rising of the Gospell With the Indians in New-England. London: Rich. Cotes for Fulk Clifton, 1647.

A Defence of the Answer made unto the Nine Questions or Positions sent from New-England, Against the Reply Thereto By . . . Mr. John Ball. London: R. Cotes for Andrew Cooke, 1648. With John Allin.

The First Principles of the Oracles of God. London: M. Simmons, 1648.

A Treatise of Ineffectual Hearing the Word. London: John Rothwell, 1652.

Journal. In *God's Plot* (above).

New Englands Lamentation for Old Englands present errours, and divisions, and their feared future desolations if not timely prevented. London: George Miller, 1645.

The Parable of the Ten Virgins. London: J. H. for John Rothwell, 1660.

The Saints Jewel, Shewing How to apply the Promise. London: John Sweeting, 1655.
The Sincere Convert. London: Humphrey Blunden, 1641.
The Soul's Invitation unto Jesus Christ. Published with *The Saints Jewel* (above).
The Sound Beleever. London: R. Dawlman, 1645.
Subjection to Christ in all his Ordinances, and Appointments, The best means to Preserve our Liberty. Published with *Ineffectual Hearing the Word* (above).
Theses Sabbaticae: Or, the Doctrine of the Sabbath. London: John Rothwell, 1649.
Thomas Shepard's Confessions. Edited by George Selement and Bruce Woolley. *Colonial Society of Massachusetts Publications* 58 (1981).
Three Valuable Pieces {Select Cases Resolved; First Principles of the Oracles of God; A Private Diary . . . }. Edited by Rev. Thomas Prince. Boston: Rogers and Fowle, 1747.
Two Questions. Boston: Bartholomew Green and John Allen, 1697.
Wine for Gospel Wantons: or, Cautions against Spiritual Drunkenness. Cambridge, Mass.: Samuel Green, 1668.

SECONDARY SOURCES

The standard biography of Shepard is John A. Albro, *The Life of Thomas Shepard* (Boston: Massachusetts Sabbath School Society, 1847). First published in the "Lives of the Chief Fathers of New England" series, it is reprinted in volume 1 of Albro's edition of Shepard's *Works.* Cotton Mather's hagiographical dramatization of Shepard, "Pastor Evangelicus: The Life of Mr. Thomas Shepard," is found in book 3 of his *Magnalia Christi Americana* (London: Thomas Parkhurst, 1702). For an annotated bibliography of secondary sources, see Thomas Werge, "Writings About Thomas Shepard, 1702–1974," in Edward J. Gallagher and Thomas Werge, *Early Puritan Writers: A Reference Guide* (Boston: G. K. Hall & Co., 1976). The following selective list includes neither articles nor, with one exception, doctoral dissertations.

Bercovitch, Sacvan. *The American Jeremiad.* Madison: University of Wisconsin Press, 1978. Forms, style, and controlling ideas in American Puritan preaching.
———. *The Puritan Origins of the American Self.* New Haven: Yale University Press, 1975. The shaping power of the Puritan experience and imagination on American thought.
Bush, Sargent, Jr. *The Writings of Thomas Hooker: Spiritual Adventure in Two Worlds.* Madison: University of Wisconsin Press, 1980. Hooker's contributions to Puritan doctrine and literature in New England.
Caldwell, Patricia. *The Puritan Conversion Narrative: The Beginnings of Amer-*

ican Expression. Cambridge: Cambridge University Press, 1983. Elements of Shepard's work in light of Puritan conversion narratives.

Colacurcio, Michael J. *The Province of Piety: Moral History in Hawthorne's Early Tales.* Cambridge, Mass.: Harvard University Press, 1984. Hawthorne's dramatic and philosophical use and critique of the Puritan mind and imagination in light of New England history.

Elliott, Emory. *Power and the Pulpit in Puritan New England.* Princeton: Princeton University Press, 1975. Homiletics and power in the ministry and audience of New England Puritanism.

Emerson, Everett H. *John Cotton.* New Haven: College and University Press with Twayne Publishers, 1965. Refers to Shepard in the setting of New England Puritan culture.

Hall, David D., ed. *The Antinomian Controversy, 1636–1638: A Documentary History.* Middletown, Conn.: Wesleyan University Press, 1968. Clarifies Shepard's vital role in the struggle between Antinomianism and orthodoxy in Massachusetts Bay.

———. *The Faithful Shepherd: A History of the New England Ministry in the Seventeenth Century.* Chapel Hill: University of North Carolina Press, 1972. Shepard's generation of New England ministers in relation to church polity and conversion experience.

Haller, William. *The Rise of Puritanism.* New York: Columbia University Press, 1938. The seminal historical consideration of the Puritan movement in England.

Holifield, E. Brooks. *The Covenant Sealed: The Development of Puritan Sacramental Theology in Old and New England, 1570–1720.* New Haven: Yale University Press, 1974. The theological and doctrinal dimensions of the Puritan understanding of the sacraments in conversion and covenant theology.

Keven, Ernest F. *The Grace of Law: A Study in Puritan Theology.* London: Carey Kingsgate Press, 1964. Law and grace in Puritan doctrine.

Levy, Babette May. *Preaching in the First Half Century of New England.* Hartford, Conn.: American Society of Church History, 1945. Shepard's style in light of Puritan homiletics.

Lewalski, Barbara. *Protestant Poetics and the Seventeenth-Century Religious Lyric.* Princeton: Princeton University Press, 1979. Protestantism in seventeenth-century thought and literature.

Lowance, Mason I. *The Language of Canaan: Metaphor and Symbol in New England from the Puritans to the Transcendentalists.* Cambridge, Mass.: Harvard University Press, 1980. Puritan language and symbolism as they shape later American ideas.

McGiffert, Michael. "Introduction." In *God's Plot* (see above). Shepard's vision and rhetoric in their Puritan setting; includes a brief analysis of earlier editions of the *Autobiography* and *Journal.*

Martz, Louis L. *The Poety of Meditation: A Study in English Religious Literature of the Seventeenth Century.* New Haven: Yale University Press, 1954. Puritan and Catholic meditation in light of meditative and sacramental tradition.

Middlekauff, Robert. *The Mathers: Three Generations of Puritan Intellectuals, 1596–1728.* New York: Oxford University Press, 1971. Shepard's relation to Hooker and others on the doctrine of conversion.

Miller, Perry. *Errand into the Wilderness.* Cambridge, Mass.: Harvard University Press, Belknap Press, 1956. Seminal essays on the mission, rhetoric, and political and apocalyptic dimensions of New England Puritanism.

———. *The New England Mind: The Seventeenth Century.* New York: Macmillan Co., 1939. The starting point for all considerations of the Puritan mind and imagination.

Mitchell, W. Fraser. *English Pulpit Oratory from Andrewes to Tillotson.* 1932. Reprint. New York: Russell & Russell, 1962. Backgrounds of Puritan sermon style.

Morgan, Edmund S. *The Puritan Family: Essays on Religious and Domestic Relations in Seventeenth-Century New England.* Boston: Trustees of the Public Library, 1944. Refers to Shepard on social and domestic subjects.

———. *Visible Saints: The History of a Puritan Idea.* New York: New York University Press, 1963. The New England conception of the church as a gathering of holy, visible saints.

Morison, Samuel Eliot. "Master Thomas Shepard." In *Builders of the Bay Colony.* Boston: Houghton Mifflin Co., 1930. Sympathetic portrayal of Shepard's life and commitments.

Murdock, Kenneth B. *Literature and Theology in Colonial New England.* Cambridge, Mass.: Harvard University Press, 1949. Considers Shepard's imagination in light of his thought and his sense of literary theory.

Olsson, Karl Arthur. "Theology and Rhetoric in the Writings of Thomas Shepard." Ph.D. dissertation, University of Chicago, 1948. Shepard's writings in light of Aristotelian rhetorical categories and Christian doctrine.

Pettit, Norman. *The Heart Prepared: Grace and Conversion in Puritan Spiritual Life.* New Haven: Yale University Press, 1966. Shepard's preparationist thought in relation to Puritan teaching on conversion.

Poulet, Georges. *Studies in Human Time.* Translated by Elliott Coleman. Baltimore: Johns Hopkins Press, 1956. The concept and dramatic interpretation of time in the Reformation and seventeenth century in light of medieval thought.

Schneider, Herbert W. *The Puritan Mind.* New York: Henry Holt, 1930. Covenant theology and the Puritan imagination.

Shea, Daniel B. *Spiritual Autobiography in Early America.* Princeton: Princeton University Press, 1968. Shepard's *Autobiography* in the setting of Puritan and Quaker literary and spiritual forms.

Shuffleton, Frank. *Thomas Hooker, 1586–1647*. Princeton: Princeton University Press, 1977. Shepard's New England setting and Hooker's central place.

Shurr, William. *Rappaccini's Children: American Writers in a Calvinist World*. Lexington: University Press of Kentucky, 1981. The Calvinist mind and imagination as influences in American literature.

Stout, Harry S. *The New England Soul: Preaching and Religious Culture in Colonial New England*. New York: Oxford University Press, 1986. Indispensable analysis of religious experience and preaching traditions in the New England context.

Tyler, Moses Coit. *A History of American Literature, 1607–1765*. 2 vols. New York: G. P. Putnam's Sons, 1878. While emphasizing the severe aspects of Shepard's works and minimizing their sacramental and reconciling dimensions, provides a lively and often sympathetic interpretation of Shepard.

Walzer, Michael. *The Revolution of the Saints: A Study in the Origins of Radical Politics*. Cambridge, Mass.: Harvard University Press, 1965. Puritan doctrine and political thought in light of the spirit of the times and earlier forms of moral order.

Watkins, Owen C. *The Puritan Experience: Studies in Spiritual Autobiography*. New York: Schocken Books, 1972. The traditions of Puritan conversion narrative and spiritual autobiography.

Whyte, Alexander. *Thomas Shepard: Pilgrim Father and Founder of Harvard: His Spiritual Experience and Experimental Preaching*. Edinburgh: Oliphant & Ferrier, 1909. Intensely personal and often idiosyncratic account of Shepard's evangelical piety, language, and example.

Index